A
Present of
Laughter

THE VIKING PRESS · NEW YORK

A Present of Laughter

Wit & Nonsense in Pictures & Verse

Edited by Bryan Holme

First published in 1982 by
The Viking Press (A Studio Book)
625 Madison Avenue
New York, N.Y. 10022
Published simultaneously
in Canada by
Penguin Books Canada Limited

Library of Congress Cataloging in Publication Data
Main entry under title:
A present of laughter.
   (A Studio book)
   Includes index.
   1.   Nonsense literature, English.   2.   Nonsense
literature, American.   I.   Holme, Bryan, 1913–
PR1111.N66P7   827'.008   81-21829
ISBN 0-670-57416-3   AACR2

Pages 168 and 169 constitute an extension of the copyright page.
Printed in the United States of America
Set in Fairfield

Many thanks to all the artists and authors who have
kindly given permission for the use of their material—
and a very special word of thanks to my editor, Mary
Velthoven, whose wisdom, wit, and great good humor
have never been more appreciated than during the
time that she helped to bring this book about. A note
of gratitude also to Stephen Sechrist, for aid in research-
ing the art of W. S. Gilbert.

Introduction

Laughter is the joyous, universal evergreen of life.
—Lincoln

If wit, as Leigh Hunt once said, is "the clash and reconcilement of incongruities; the meeting of extremes round a corner," laughter might be said to be the neutralizing force by which incongruities are pleasantly resolved. The alternative is to cry, which no one wants to do if he can possibly help it, although to cry with laughter is something else again. Pure unadulterated laughter, together with the capacity to provoke it at all well, surely is one of God's greatest gifts to man.

The unexpected, the clever, the absurd, are equally likely to make us laugh. Harmless accidents can, too: the slip of a tongue might cause "a bog darking" to come out instead of "a dog barking," or, as a lady was heard saying a little testily to her husband, "Aren't we poking at cross tortoises?" When mutual laughter followed her remark, obviously "talking at cross purposes" was no longer an issue.

Wit may be the keenest tool in provoking laughter, yet as Sheridan pointed out, "There's no possibility of being witty without a little ill nature; the malice of a good thing is the barb that makes it stick." On the other hand, artful nonsense or brilliant tommyrot never hurt a soul; it's the lighthearted kind of intellectual diet that brightens a rainy day.

According to an unwritten rule, a work of nonsense must not be entirely true, neither must it be completely false. An author left to tread the light fantastic between these two opposites might be drawn toward sheer nonsense, or, if more thoughtfully inclined, might tend the other way, philosophizing about life in some teasing kind of prose or rhyme.

On the face of it, writing nonsense would seem very easy; perhaps not quite as easy as talking nonsense—which cynics would have us believe most of the world spends most of its time doing—but very nearly so. Yet, first-rate nonsense is as difficult to write as fine poetry.

The practice of nonsense was recognized as a skilled art in Roman times and probably earlier. The Romans had their humorous *scurrae* and *moriones,* and medieval kings and princes found an equivalent in the court fool, or jester, a profession which rose to its height in England under the Tudors. The perfect jester combined the antics of a clown with the wit of a sage, the tact of a diplomat, and the instincts of a prophet; he was able to make known to his master, comically yet objectively, the direction in which public opinion and the winds of fate might be blowing. The Fool advises King Lear:

> That lord, that counselled thee
> > To give away thy land,
> Come place him here by me—
> > Do thou for him stand.
> The sweet and bitter fool
> > Will presently appear;
> The one in motley here,
> > The other found out there.

and makes the best of his own situation:

> He that has and a little tiny wit,
> > With, heigh-ho, the wind and the rain,
> Must make content with his fortunes fit
> > Though the rain it raineth every day.

The shrewd politician, occasionally stealing a leaf from the clever fool's book, would find in nonsense or in doubletalk an artful way of parrying an awkward question or veiling an embarrassing truth. In the eighteenth century, when the profession of jester had all but died out, England's great statesman William Pitt was heard to exclaim, "Don't tell me of man's being able to talk sense; everyone can talk sense. Can he talk nonsense?" To do so effectively always took not merely cleverness, but brilliance.

In this book, a point has been made of reviving lesser-known works of wit and nonsense, but a well-rounded treasury calls for the familiar, too. Inevitably, therefore, some of the best of Edward Lear is included, along with samplings of the wit of Hilaire Belloc and of Lewis Carroll, who has probably made nonsense seem more like sense than anyone else ever has.

For pure nonsense, Carroll's *Through the Looking Glass* is perhaps even more remarkable than *Alice in Wonderland,* not only for the popular "The Walrus and the Carpenter," but for that masterpiece of absolute meaninglessness that begins:

> 'Twas brillig, and the slithy toves
> > Did gyre and gimble in the wabe;
> All mimsy were the borogroves,
> > And the mome raths outgrabe.

Although Carroll maintained that every idea and nearly every word of dialogue in his two *Alice* books "came of itself," it is sometimes argued that the full "Jabberwocky" could not have been quite that spontaneous. There never has been any question, however, that it is a work of pure genius.

Some of the best nonsense comes about quite by chance; a thought arising as if from nowhere floats merrily around and out of the top of one's head, or a sketch or doodle appears magically on paper as if the tip of the pencil had conjured it there. It is not entirely impossible to visualize Shakespeare sitting back a little wearily between laboring over the dialogue of *As You Like It,* giving a relaxing little sigh and finding that out of that little sigh came an unpremeditated "With a hey, and a ho, and a hey nonino."

An equally famous refrain that ripples merrily along is:

> With a rowley-powley, gammon and spinach,
> Heigho, says Anthony Rowley!

When or where the author of "A Frog He Would A-Wooing Go" wrote these lines nobody will ever know (versions of it were current in Shakespeare's time) but the reason why he chose to use "gammon" instead of the more common word for the same general area of the hapless pig is obvious, for to recite "ham and spinach" instead of "gammon and spinach" would be to destroy both the rhythm and the charm of the verse. There is a well-founded theory that the refrain "rowley-powley, gammon and spinach" evolved out of a witch's incantation, not of the "bubble, bubble, toil and trouble" variety, but out of prognostications of courtship and marriage in which food, fertility herbs, and happy mumbo-jumbo somehow or other got rolled into a rollicking rhyme.

A very different kind of nonsense stems from the irregularities of the English language, those inconsistencies in the spelling, meaning, and pronunciation of words that at times drive the foreign student to distraction. Why, for instance, should the word "mean" have two quite different meanings, and share the same pronunciation as "mien," which means something else again?

Were words to be spelled exactly as pronounced, one might come up with something like:

> "I thort the nerce in the hospittle so luvly I
> offered her wun of my favret choklets"

Which strangely sounds Cockney without being so.

Geoffrey Willans, past master of schoolboy nonsense, has filled his "Molesworth" books with all sorts of rebellious delicacies. In *Whizz for Atoms* Molesworth remarks:

> "Everyone kno wot we are like now you hav only to look around and see it is ghastly stuff. But wot of the future?"

In *A Spaniard in the Works* John Lennon also took impish delight in spelling some words as they might be pronounced and misspelling others—aided, it would seem, by happy slips on the keys of the typewriter. A case in point is "Araminta Ditch," who was always "larfing":

> One date Araminta rose up out of her duffle bed, larfing as usual with that insage larf peojle had come to know her form.
> 'Hee! hee! hee!' She larfed all the way down to breakfart.
> 'Hee! hee! hee' She gurgled over the morman papiers.
> 'Hee! hee! hee!' Continue Araminta on the buzz to wirk.
> This pubbled the passages and condoctor equally both. 'Why is that boot larfing all the time?' Inqueered an elderberry passengeorge who trabelled regularge on that roof and had a write to know.

Writing about the appreciation of nonsense a little after the turn of the century, the poet and anthologist Carolyn Wells maintained that "the majority of the reading world does not appreciate or enjoy nonsense and this, again, is consequent upon their inability to discriminate between nonsense of integral merit and simple chaff.

> A jest's prosperity lies in the ear
> Of him that hears it, never in the tongue
> Of him that makes it.

and a sense of nonsense is as distinct a part of our mentality as a sense of humor, being by no means identical therewith."

There are examples of literature nonsensical in form, or bordering on it, that make more of a point than many a piece of "serious" prose. Paul West's "The Cumberbunce" (page 142) fits into this category, as does Joseph Ashby-Sterry's "Kindness to Animals" (page 99) as well as a poem by William Mackworth Praed called "A Song of Impossibilities," in which the following verse appears:

> When peers from telling money shrink,
>   Or monks from telling lies;
> When hydrogen begins to sink,
>   Or Grecian scrip to rise;
> When German poets cease to dream,
>   Americans to guess;
> When Freedom sheds her holy beam
>   On Negroes, and the Press;
> When there is any fear of Rome,
>   Or any hope of Spain;
> When Ireland is a happy home,
>   I may be yours again!

More closely identified with nonsense, perhaps, than any other literature is the limerick. Although Edward Lear, the so-called parent of modern nonsense writers, was not the originator of the limerick form, he was so expert at this light kind of stanza and so prolific—over two hundred of his limericks were published before he died in 1888—that he became the unchallenged leader in the field.

We must not forget, however, that first and foremost Lear was an artist, one sufficiently qualified to serve as Queen Victoria's drawing master. Only later did Lear become famous, not for his serious work but, quite by chance, for his nonsense. Inspired by a number of limericks he came across one day in an unknown author's book, Lear started making up and illustrating his own verses solely, at first, to amuse the grandchildren of the earl of Derby, to whose estate he had been invited in 1832 in order to make a visual record of the earl's menagerie. Fourteen years later the London publisher Thomas MacLean, recognizing the commercial possibilities of Lear's limericks, published *A Book of Nonsense*, which became such a success that no less than thirty editions were printed in the author's lifetime alone.

Although Lear drew with a much freer hand than either the English caricaturist and illustrator George Cruikshank or the great French illustrator of human foibles known as Grandville, something of these two senior nineteenth-century artists is recognizable in his work. Cruikshank and Grandville very naturally take their places in these pages along with Lear and a host of others— Charles Bennett, Randolph Caldecott, Walter Crane, Leslie Brooks, James Thurber and Ronald Searle included—who have kept nonsense visually and sublimely alive to this day.

A wise person once remarked, "You can only laugh at life—unless you want to cry, and on the whole I prefer to laugh, don't you?" This book is dedicated to all those who have been able to set such an excellent example.

Bryan Holme

11

A
Present of
Laughter

BUZ, QUOTH THE BLUE FLY

Buz, quoth the blue fly,
      Hum, quoth the bee,
Buz and hum they cry,
      And so do we:
In his ear, in his nose, thus, do you see?
He ate the dormouse, else it was he.

Ben Jonson (1573?–1637)

MARTIN TO HIS MAN

Martin said to his man,
    Fie! man, fie!
Oh, Martin said to his man,
    Who's the fool now?
Martin said to his man,
Fill thou the cup, and I the can;
Thou hast well drunken, man:
    Who's the fool now?

I see a sheep shearing corn,
    Fie! man, fie!
I see a sheep shearing corn,
    Who's the fool now?
I see a sheep shearing corn,
And a cuckoo blow his horn;
Thou hast well drunken, man:
    Who's the fool now?

I see a man in the moon,
    Fie! man, fie!
I see a man in the moon,
    Who's the fool now?

I see a man in the moon,
Clouting of St. Peter's shoon,
Thou hast well drunken, man:
    Who's the fool now?

I see a goose ring a hog,
    Fie! man, fie!
I see a goose ring a hog,
    Who's the fool now?
I see a goose ring a hog,
And a snail that bit a dog;
Thou hast well drunken, man:
    Who's the fool now?

I see a mouse catch the cat,
    Fie! man, fie!
I see a mouse catch the cat,
    Who's the fool now?
I see a mouse catch the cat,
And the cheese to eat the rat;
Thou hast well drunken, man:
    Who's the fool now?

From Deuteromelia,
printed in the reign of James I

A TERNARIE OF LITTLES,
UPON A PIPKIN OF JELLIE
SENT TO A LADY

A little Saint best fits a little Shrine,
A little prop best fits a little Vine,
As my small Cruse best fits my little Wine.

A little Seed best fits a little Soyle,
A little Trade best fits a little Toyle:
As my small Jarre best fits my little Oyle.

A little Bin best fits a little Bread,
A little Garland fits a little Head:
As my small stuffe best fits my little Shed.

A little Hearth best fits a little Fire,
A little Chappell fits a little Quire,
As my small Bell best fits my little Spire.

A little streame best fits a little Boat;
A little lead best fits a little Float;
As my small Pipe best fits my little note.

A little meat best fits a little bellie,
As sweetly Lady, give me leave to tell ye,
This little Pipkin fits this little Jellie.

Robert Herrick (1591–1674)

LIMERICK

There was an old man of Tyre
Who constantly sat on the fire
When asked "is it hot?"
He replied "no it's not,
For I'm James Winterbotham Esquire."

Anonymous

ON THE OXFORD CARRIER

Here lieth one, who did most truly prove
That he could never die while he could move;
So hung his destiny never to rot
While he might still jog on and keep his trot;
Made of sphere metal, never to decay
Until his revolution was at stay.
Time numbers motion, yet (without a crime
'Gainst old truth) motion number'd out his time,
And like an engine moved with wheel and weight,
His principles being ceased, he ended straight.
Rest, that gives all men life, gave him his death,
And too much breathing put him out of breath;
Nor were it contradiction to affirm,
Too long vacation hasten'd on his term.
Merely to drive the time away he sicken'd,
Fainted, and died, nor would with ale be quicken'd;
"Nay," quoth he, on his swooning bed outstretch'd,
"If I mayn't carry, sure I'll ne'er be fetch'd,
But vow, though the cross doctors all stood hearers,
For one carrier put down to make six bearers."
Ease was his chief disease; and to judge right,
He died for heaviness that his cart went light:
His leisure told him that his time was come,
And lack of load made his life burdensome.
That even to his last breath (there be that say't),
As he were press'd to death, he cried, "More weight";
But, had his doings lasted as they were,
He had been an immortal carrier.
Obedient to the moon he spent his date
In course reciprocal, and had his fate
Link'd to the mutual flowing of the seas,
Yet (strange to think) his wane was his increase:
His letters are deliver'd all, and gone,
Only remains the superscription.

John Milton (1608–1674)

16

NONSENSE

Oh that my lungs could bleat like butter'd pease;
    But bleating of my lungs hath caught the itch,
And are as mangy as the Irish seas
    That doth engender windmills on a bitch.

I grant that rainbowes being lull'd asleep,
    Snort like a woodknife in a lady's eyes;
Which makes her grieve to see a pudding creep,
    For creeping puddings only please the wise.

Not that a hard-row'd herring should presume
    To swing a tythe pig in a cateskin purse;
For fear the hailstones which did fall at Rome,
    By lessening of the fault should make it worse.

For 't is most certain winter woolsacks grow
    From geese to swans if men could keep them so,
Till that the sheep shorn planets gave the hint
    To pickle pancakes in Geneva print.

Some men there were that did suppose the skie
    Was made of carbonado'd antidotes;
But my opinion is, a whale's left eye,
    Need not be coynéd all King Harry groates.

The reason's plain, for Charon's western barge
    Running a tilt at the subjunctive mood,
Beckoned to Bednal Green, and gave him charge
    To fasten padlocks with Antarctic food.

The end will be the mill ponds must be laded,
    To fish for white pots in a country dance;
So they that suffered wrong and were upbraided
    Shall be made friends in a left-handed trance.

Anonymous (1617)

A CHRONICLE

Once—but no matter when—
  There lived—no matter where—
A man, whose name—but then
  I need not that declare.

He—well, he had been born,
  And so he was alive;
His age—I details scorn—
  Was somethingty and five.

He lived—how many years
  I truly can't decide;
But this one fact appears
  He lived—until he died.

"He died," I have averred,
  But cannot prove 't was so,
But that he was interred,
  At any rate, I know.

I fancy he'd a son,
  I hear he had a wife:

Perhaps he 'd more than one,
  I know not, on my life!

But whether he was rich,
  Or whether he was poor,
Or neither—both—or which,
  I cannot say, I'm sure.

I can't recall his name,
  Or what he used to do:
But then—well, such is fame!
  'T will so serve me and you.

And that is why I thus,
  About this unknown man
Would fain create a fuss,
  To rescue, if I can.

From dark oblivion's blow,
  Some record of his lot:
But, ah! I do not know
  Who—where—when—why—or what.

MORAL

In this brief pedigree
  A moral we should find—
But what it ought to be
  Has quite escaped my mind!

Anonymous

18

THE SLUGGARD

'Tis the voice of the sluggard; I heard him complain,
"You have waked me too soon, I must slumber again."
As the door on its hinges, so he on his bed,
Turns his sides and his shoulders and his heavy head.

"A little more sleep and a little more slumber";
Thus he wastes half his days and his hours without number;
And when he gets up, he sits folding his hands,
Or walks about saunt'ring, or trifling he stands.

I pass'd by his garden, and saw the wild briar,
The thorn and the thistle grow broader and higher;
The clothes that hang on him are turning to rags;
And his money still wastes, till he starves or he begs.

I made him a visit, still hoping to find
He had took better care for improving his mind:
He told me his dreams, talked of eating and drinking;
But he scarce reads his Bible, and never loves thinking.

Isaac Watts (1674–1748)

IF——

If all the world were paper,
    And all the sea were ink;
If all the trees were bread and cheese,
    How should we do for drink?

If all the world were sand,
    Oh then what should we lack'o?
If as they say there were no clay,
    How should we take tobacco?

If all our vessels ran,
    If none but had a crack;
If Spanish apes ate all the grapes,
    How should we do for sack?

If all the world were men,
    And men lived all in trenches,
And there were none but we alone,
    How should we do for wenches?

If friars had no bald pates,
    Nor nuns had no dark cloisters;
If all the seas were beans and peas,
    How should we do for oysters?

If all things were eternal,
    And nothing their end bringing;
If this should be, then how should we
    Here make an end of singing?

Anonymous (1641)

THE AUTHOR TO HER BOOK

Thou ill-formed offspring of my feeble brain,
Who after birth did'st by my side remain,
Till snatched from thence by friends, less wise than true,
Who thee abroad exposed to public view;
Made thee in rags, halting, to the press to trudge,
Where errors were not lessened, all may judge.
At thy return my blushing was not small,
My rambling brat (in print) should mother call;
I cast thee by as one unfit for light,
Thy visage was so irksome in my sight;
Yet being mine own, at length affection would
Thy blemishes amend, if so I could:
I washed thy face, but more defects I saw,
And rubbing off a spot, still made a flaw.
I stretched thy joints to make thee even feet,
Yet still thou run'st more hobbling than is meet;
In better dress to trim thee was my mind,
But nought save homespun cloth, in the house I find.
In this array, 'mongst vulgars may'st thou roam;
In criticks hands beware thou dost not come;
And take thy way where yet thou are not known.
If for thy Father asked, say thou had'st none;
And for thy Mother, she alas is poor,
Which caused her thus to send thee out of door.

Samuel Sewall (1652–1730)

PUER EX JERSEY

Puer ex Jersey   Ille approaches
Iens ad school;   O magnus sorrow!
Vidit in meadow,   Puer it skyward.
Infestum mule.   Funus ad morrow.

MORAL

Qui vidit a thing
Non ei well-known,
Est bene for him
Relinqui id alone.

Anonymous

MASTER AND MAN

Master I have, and I am his man,
    Gallop a dreary dun;
Master I have, and I am his man,
And I'll get a wife as fast as I can;
With a heighly gaily gamberally,
    Higgledy piggledy, niggledy, niggledy,
    Gallop a dreary dun.

Anonymous

LINES BY A PERSON OF QUALITY

Fluttering spread thy purple pinions,
    Gentle Cupid, o'er my heart,
I a slave in thy dominions,
    Nature must give way to art.

Mild Arcadians, ever blooming,
    Nightly nodding o'er your flocks,
See my weary days consuming,
    All beneath yon flowery rocks.

Thus the Cyprian goddess weeping,
    Mourned Adonis, darling youth:
Him the boar, in silence creeping,
    Gored with unrelenting tooth.

Cynthia, tune harmonious numbers;
    Fair Discretion, tune the lyre;
Soothe my ever-waking slumbers;
    Bright Apollo, lend thy choir.

Gloomy Pluto, king of terrors,
    Armed in adamantine chains,
Lead me to the crystal mirrors,
    Watering soft Elysian plains.

Mournful Cypress, verdant willow,
    Gilding my Aurelia's brows,
Morpheus, hovering o'er my pillow,
    Hear me pay my dying vows.

Melancholy, smooth Mæander,
    Swiftly purling in a round,
On thy margin lovers wander
    With thy flowery chaplets crowned.

Thus when Philomela, drooping,
    Softly seeks her silent mate,
So the bird of Juno stooping;
    Melody resigns to fate.

Alexander Pope (1688–1744)

THE POWER OF MUSIC

When Orpheus went down to the regions below,
    Which men are forbidden to see,
He turned up his lyre, as old histories show,
    To set his Eurydice free.

All hell was astonished a person so wise
    Should rashly endanger his life,
And venture so far—but how vast their surprise
    When they heard that he came for his wife.

To find out a punishment due to his fault
    Old Pluto had puzzled his brain;
But hell had no torments sufficient, he thought,
    So he gave him his wife back again.

But pity succeeding found place in his heart,
    And, pleased with his playing so well,
He took her again in reward of his art;
    Such power hath music in hell!

Thomas Lisle (1709–1767)

KING ARTHUR

When good King Arthur ruled the land,
    He was a goodly king:
He stole three pecks of barley meal,
    To make a bag-pudding.

A bag-pudding the king did make,
    And stuffed it well with plums;
And in it put great lumps of fat,
    As big as my two thumbs.

The king and queen did eat thereof,
    And noblemen beside;
And what they could not eat that night,
    The queen next morning fried.

Anonymous

IMPROMPTU

Jack, eating rotten cheese, did say,
Like Samson I my thousands slay:
I vow, quoth Roger, so you do,
And with the selfsame weapon too.

Benjamin Franklin (1706–1790)

Randolph Caldecott (1846–1886)

THE GRAND PANJANDRUM

"So she went into the garden to cut a cabbage-leaf to make an apple-pie; and at the same time a great she-bear, coming up the street, pops its head into the shop: 'What! no soap?' So he died, and she very imprudently married the Barber. And there were present the Picninnies, and the Joblillies, and the Garyalies, and the grand Panjandrum himself, with the little round button at top. And they all fell to playing the game of catch-as-catch-can, till the gunpowder ran out at the heels of their boots."

Samuel Foote (1720–1777)

23

THE ELDERLY GENTLEMAN

By the side of a murmuring stream an elderly gentleman sat.
On the top of his head was a wig, and a-top of his wig was his hat.

The wind it blew high and blew strong, as the elderly gentleman sat;
And bore from his head in a trice, and plunged in the river his hat.

The gentleman then took his cane which lay by his side as he sat;
And he dropped in the river his wig, in attempting to get out his hat.

His breast it grew cold with despair, and full in his eye madness sat;
So he flung in the river his cane to swim with his wig, and his hat.

Cool reflection at last came across while this elderly gentleman sat;
So he thought he would follow the stream and look for his cane, wig, and hat.

His head being thicker than common, o'er-balanced the rest of his fat;
And in plumped this son of a woman to follow his wig, cane, and hat.

George Canning (1770–1827)

LAZY BONES

Lazy-bones, lazy-bones, wake up and peep!
The cat's in the cupboard, your mother's asleep.
There you sit snoring, forgetting her ills;
Who is to give her her Bolus and Pills?
Twenty fine Angels must come into town,
All for to help you to make your new gown:
Dainty aerial Spinsters and Singers;
Aren't you ashamed to employ such white fingers?
Delicate hands, unaccustom'd to reels,
To set 'em working a poor body's wheels?
Why they came down is to me all a riddle,
And left Hallelujah broke off in the middle:
Jove's Court, and the Presence angelical, cut—
To eke out the work of a lazy young slut.
Angel-duck, Angel-duck, winged and silly,
Pouring a watering-pot over a lily,
Gardener gratuitous, careless of pelf,
Leave her to water her lily herself,
Or to neglect it to death if she chuse it:
Remember the loss is her own if she lose it.

Charles Lamb (1775–1834)

INFANT SORROW

My mother groaned, my father wept;
Into the dangerous world I leapt;
Helpless, naked, piping loud,
Like a fiend hid in a cloud.

Struggling in my father's hands,
Striving against my swaddling-bands,
Bound and weary, I thought best
To sulk upon my mother's breast.

William Blake (1757–1827)

GLEE—THE GHOSTS

In life three ghostly friars were we,
And now three friarly ghosts we be.
Around our shadowy table placed,
The spectral bowl before us floats;
With wine that none but ghosts can taste,
We wash our unsubstantial throats.
Three merry ghosts—three merry ghosts—three merry ghosts are we:
Let the ocean be Port, and we'll think it good sport
To be laid in that Red Sea.

With songs that jovial spectres chaunt,
Our old refectory still we haunt.
The traveller hears our midnight mirth:
"O list!" he cries, "the haunted choir!
The merriest ghost that walks the earth,
Is sure the ghost of a ghostly friar."
Three merry ghosts—three merry ghosts—three merry ghosts are we:
Let the ocean be Port, and we'll think it good sport
To be laid in that Red Sea.

Thomas Love Peacock (1785–1866)

If a man who turnips cries,
Cry not when his father dies,
'T is a proof that he would rather
Have a turnip than a father.

Samuel Johnson (1709–1784)

THREE·WISE
MEN OF GOTHAM

BYAM
SHAW

THE WISE MEN OF GOTHAM

In a bowl to sea went wise men three,
    On a brilliant night of June:
They carried a net, and their hearts were set
    On fishing up the Moon.

The sea was calm, the air was balm,
    Not a breath stirred low or high,
And the Moon, I trow, lay as bright below,
    And as round as in the sky.

The wise men with the current went,
    Nor paddle nor oar had they,
And still as the grave they went on the wave,
    That they might not disturb their prey.

Far, far at sea were the wise men three,
    When their fishing net they threw;
And at their throw the Moon below
    In a thousand fragments flew.

They drew in their net, it was empty and wet,
    And they had lost their pain,
Soon ceased the play of each dancing ray,
    And the image was round again.

Three times they threw, three times they drew,
    And all the while were mute;
And ever anew their wonder grew,
    Till they could not but dispute.

The three wise men got home again
    To their children and their wives:
But touching their trip and their net's vain dip
    They disputed all their lives.

The wise men three could never agree
    Why they missed their promised boon;
They agreed alone that their net they had thrown,
    And they had not caught the Moon.

Thomas Love Peacock (1785–1866)
Illustration by Byam Shaw (1872–1919)

CLOCK-A-CLAY

In the cowslip pips I lie
Hidden from the buzzing fly,
While green grass beneath me lies
Pearled with dew like fishes' eyes,
Here I lie, a clock-a-clay,
Waiting for the time of day.

While grassy forests quake surprise,
And the wild wind sobs and sighs,
My gold home rocks as like to fall
On its pillar green and tall;
When the parting rain drives by
Clock-a-clay keeps warm and dry.

Day by day and night by night
All the week I hide from sight.
In the cowslip pips I lie,
In rain and dew still warm and dry.
Day and night, and night and day,
Red, black-spotted clock-a-clay.

My home shakes in wind and showers,
Pale green pillar topped with flowers,
Bending at the wild wind's breath
Till I touch the grass beneath;
Here I live, lone clock-a-clay,
Watching for the time of day.

John Clare (1793–1864)

PARSON GRAY

A quiet home had Parson Gray,
    Secluded in a vale;
His daughters all were feminine,
    And all his sons were male.

How faithfully did Parson Gray
    The bread of life dispense—
Well "posted" in theology,
    And post and rail his fence.

'Gainst all the vices of the age
    He manfully did battle;
His chickens were a biped breed,
    And quadruped his cattle.

No clock more punctually went,
    He ne'er delayed a minute—
Nor ever empty was his purse,
    When he had money in it.

His piety was ne'er denied;
    His truths hit saint and sinner;
At morn he always breakfasted;
    He always dined at dinner.

He ne'er by any luck was grieved,
    By any care perplexed—
No filcher he, though when he preached,
    He always "took" a text.

As faithful characters he drew
    As mortal ever saw;
But ah! poor parson! when he died,
    His breath he could not draw!

Oliver Goldsmith (1728–1774)

ON COMMUNISTS

What is a Communist? One who has yearnings
For equal division of unequal earnings;
Idler or bungler, or both, he is willing
To fork out his penny and pocket your shilling.

Ebenezer Elliott (1781–1849)

NONSENSE

Good reader, if you e'er have seen,
    When Phœbus hastens to his pillow,
        The mermaids with their tresses green
    Dancing upon the western billow;
        If you have seen at twilight dim,
        When the lone spirit's vesper hymn
    Floats wild along the winding shore,
The fairy train their ringlets weave
    Glancing along the spangled green; —
        If you have seen all this, and more,
    God bless me! what a deal you've seen!

Thomas Moore (1779–1852)

A LOVE-SONG BY A LUNATIC

There's not a spider in the sky,
    There's not a glowworm in the sea,
There's not a crab that soars on high,
    But bids me dream, dear maid, of thee!

When watery Phœbus ploughs the main,
    When fiery Luna gilds the lea,
As flies run up the window-pane,
    So fly my thoughts, dear love, to thee!

Anonymous

A SONG ABOUT MYSELF

From a letter to Fanny Keats

There was a naughty Boy,
    A naughty boy was he,
He would not stop at home,
    He could not quiet be—
        He took
        In his Knapsack
        A Book
        Full of vowels
        And a shirt
        With some towels—
        A slight cap
        For night cap—
        A hair brush,
        Comb ditto,
        New Stockings
        For old ones
        Would split O!
        This Knapsack
        Tight at's back
        He rivetted close
And followed his Nose
        To the North,
        To the North,
And follow'd his nose to the North.

There was a naughty boy
    And a naughty boy was he,
For nothing would he do
    But scribble poetry—
        He took
        An ink stand
        In his hand
        And a Pen
        Big as ten
        In the other.
        And away
        In a Pother
        He ran
        To the mountains
        And fountains
        And ghostes
        And Postes
        And witches
        And ditches
        And wrote
        In his coat
        When the weather
        Was cool,
        Fear of gout,
        And without
        When the weather
        Was warm—
        Och, the charm
        When we choose
To follow one's nose
        To the North,
        To the North,
To follow one's nose to the North!

There was a naughty boy
    And a naughty boy was he,
He kept little fishes
    In washing tubs three
        In spite
        Of the might
        Of the Maid
        Nor affraid
        Of his Granny-good—
        He often would
        Hurly burly
        Get up early
        And go
        By hook or crook
        To the brook
        And bring home
        Miller's thumb,
        Tittlebat
        Not over fat,
        Minnows small
        As the stall
        Of a glove,
        Not above
        The size
        Of a nice
        Little Baby's
        Little fingers—
        O he made
        'Twas his trade
Of Fish a pretty Kettle
    A Kettle—a Kettle
Of Fish a pretty Kettle
    A Kettle!

There was a naughty Boy,
    And a naughty boy was he,
He ran away to Scotland
    The people for to see—
        Then he found
        That the ground
        Was as hard,
        That a yard
        Was as long,
        That a song
        Was as merry,
        That a cherry
        Was as red—
        That lead
        Was as weighty,
        That fourscore
        Was as eighty,
        That a door
        Was as wooden
        As in England—
So he stood in
    His shoes and he wonder'd,
    He wonder'd,
He stood in
    His shoes and he wonder'd.

John Keats (1795–1821)

THE FAIRIES

Up the airy mountain,
　　Down the rushy glen,
We daren't go a-hunting
　　For fear of little men.
Wee folk, good folk,
　　Trooping all together;
Green jacket, red cap,
　　And white owl's feather!

Down along the rocky shore
　　Some make their home—
They live on crispy pancakes
　　Of yellow tide-foam;
Some in the reeds
　　Of the black mountain-lake,
With frogs for their watch-dogs,
　　All night awake.

High on the hill-top
　　The old King sits;
He is now so old and grey,
　　He's nigh lost his wits.

With a bridge of white mist
　　Columbkill he crosses,
On his stately journeys
　　From Slieveleague to Rosses;
Or going up with music
　　On cold starry nights,
To sup with the Queen
　　Of the gay Northern Lights.

They stole little Bridget
　　For seven years long;
When she came down again,
　　Her friends were all gone.
They took her lightly back,
　　Between the night and morrow;
They thought that she was fast asleep,
　　But she was dead with sorrow.
They have kept her ever since
　　Deep within the lake,
On a bed of flag-leaves,
　　Watching till she wake.

William Allingham (1824–1889)

Some Fairy Knights, too, came over the border, and they fought with spears, riding Beetles and Grasshoppers, instead of horses.

Scenes from The Princess Nobody *by Andrew Lang (1844–1912)*

Illustrations from In Fairyland *by Richard Doyle (1824–1883)*

Here is the Prince Comical (you see he is not very handsome!) and here is the king so sound asleep.

"Try to waken him," said the Beetle; "just try."

So the prince tried to waken the King, but it was of no use.

THE PLAGIARIST *like the magpie who clothes himself in plumes borrowed from others.*

SWIMMING SCHOOL.
Grandville (1803–1847)

THE SORROWS OF WERTHER

Werther had a love for Charlotte
    Such as words could never utter;
Would you know how first he met her?
    She was cutting bread and butter.

Charlotte was a married lady,
    And a moral man was Werther,
And for all the wealth of Indies,
    Would do nothing for to hurt her.

So he sigh'd and pined and ogled,
    And his passion boil'd and bubbled,
Till he blew his silly brains out,
    And no more was by it troubled.

Charlotte, having seen his body
    Borne before her on a shutter,
Like a well-conducted person,
    Went on cutting bread and butter.

William Makepeace Thackeray (1811–1863)

MINNIE AND WINNIE

Minnie and Winnie
    Slept in a shell.
Sleep, little ladies!
    And they slept well.

Pink was the shell within,
    Silver without;
Sounds of the great sea
    Wandered about.

Sleep little ladies!
    Wake not soon!
Echo on echo
    Dies to the moon.

Two bright stars
    Peep'd into the shell,
What are they dreaming of?
    Who can tell?

Started a green linnet
    Out of the croft;
Wake, little ladies,
    The sun is aloft!

Alfred, Lord Tennyson
(1809–1892)

A SPLENDID SPREAD.

George Cruikshank (1792–1878)

UPRISING SEE THE FITFUL LARK

Uprising see the fitful lark
    Unfold his pinion to the stream;
The pensive watch-dog's mellow bark
    O'ershades yon cottage like a dream:
The playful duck and warbling bee
Hop gayly on, from tree to tree!

How calmly could my spirit rest
    Beneath yon primrose bell so blue,
And watch those airy oxen drest
    In every tint of pearling hue!
As on they hurl the gladsome plough,
While fairy zephyrs deck each brow!

Anonymous

APRIL

The April winds are magical
And thrill our tuneful frames;
The garden walks are passional
To bachelors and dames.
The hedge is gemmed with diamonds,
The air with Cupids full,
The cobweb clues of Rosamond
Guide lovers to the pool.
Each dimple in the water,
Each leaf that shades the rock

Can cozen, pique and flatter,
Can parley and provoke.
Goodfellow, Puck and goblins,
Know more than any book.
Down with your doleful problems,
And court the sunny brook.
The south-winds are quick-witted,
The schools are sad and slow,
The masters quite omitted
The lore we care to know.

Ralph Waldo Emerson (1803–1882)

FELLOWS OF THE ZOOLOGICAL SOCIETY.   *George Cruikshank* (1792–1878)

SCIENCE UNDER DIVERS FORMS.   *George Cruikshank* (1792–1878)

A LITERARY BULL.   *George Cruikshank* (1792–1878)

THE FLAMINGO

Inspired by reading a chorus of spirits in a German play

FIRST VOICE

Oh! tell me have you ever seen a red, long-leg'd Flamingo?
Oh! tell me have you ever yet seen him the water in go?

SECOND VOICE

Oh! yes at Bowling-Green I've seen a red long-leg'd Flamingo,
Oh! yes at Bowling-Green I've there seen him the water in go.

FIRST VOICE

Oh! tell me did you ever see a bird so funny stand-o
When forth he from the water comes and gets upon the land-o?

SECOND VOICE

No! in my life I ne'er did see a bird so funny stand-o
When forth he from the water comes and gets upon the land-o.

FIRST VOICE

He has a leg some three feet long, or near it, so they say, Sir.
Stiff upon one alone he stands, t'other he stows away, Sir.

SECOND VOICE

And what an ugly head he's got! I wonder that he'd wear it.
But rather *more* I wonder that his long, thin neck can bear it.

FIRST VOICE

And think, this length of neck and legs (no doubt they have their uses)
Are members of a little frame, much smaller than a goose's!

BOTH

Oh! isn't he a curious bird, that red, long-leg'd Flamingo?
A water bird, a gawky bird, a sing'lar bird, by jingo!

Lewis Gaylord Clark (1808–1873)

"THERE IS NO GOD,"
THE WICKED SAITH

"There is no God," the wicked saith,
    "And truly it's a blessing,
For what he might have done with us
    It's better only guessing."

"There is no God," a youngster thinks,
    "Or really, if there may be,
He surely didn't mean a man
    Always to be a baby."

"There is no God, or if there is,"
    The tradesman thinks, " 'twere funny
If he should take it ill in me
    To make a little money."

"Whether there be," the rich man says,
    "It matters very little,
For I and mine, thank somebody,
    And are not in want of victual."

Some others, also, to themselves
    Who scarce so much as doubt it,
Think there is none, when they are well,
    And do not think about it.

But country folks who live beneath
    The shadow of the steeple;
The parson and the parson's wife,
    And mostly married people;

Youths green and happy in first love,
    So thankful for illusion;
And men caught out in what the world
    Calls guilt, in first confusion;

And almost everyone when age,
    Disease, or sorrows strike him,
Inclines to think there is a God,
    Or something very like Him.

Arthur Hugh Clough (1819–1861)

EPIGRAPH TO
NEW POEMS, 1867

Though the Muse be gone away,
Though she move not earth today,
Souls, erewhile who caught her word
Ah, still harp on what they heard.

Matthew Arnold (1822–1888)

LOWELL

There is Lowell, who's striving Parnassus to climb
With a whole bale of *isms* tied together with rhyme,
He might get on alone, spite of brambles and boulders,
But he can't with that bundle he has on his shoulders,
The top of the hill he will ne'er come nigh reaching
Till he learns the distinction 'twixt singing and preaching;
His lyre has some chords that would ring pretty well,
But he'd rather by half make a drum of the shell,
And rattle away till he's old as Methusalem,
At the head of a march to the last new Jerusalem.

James Russell Lowell (1819–1891)

WHEN MOONLIKE ORE THE
HAZURE SEAS

When moonlike ore the hazure seas
    In soft effulgence swells,
When silver jewls and balmy breaze
    Bend down the Lily's bells;
When calm and deap, the rosy sleap
    Has lapt your soal in dreems,
R Hangeline! R lady mine!
    Dost thou remember Jeames?

I mark thee in the Marble all,
    Where England's loveliest shine—
I say the fairest of them hall
    Is Lady Hangeline.

My soal, in desolate eclipse,
    With recollection teems—
And then I hask, with weeping lips,
    Dost thou remember Jeames?

Away! I may not tell thee hall
    This soughring heart endures—
There is a lonely sperrit-call
    That Sorrow never cures;
There is a little, little Star,
    That still above me beams;
It is the Star of Hope—but ar!
    Dost thou remember Jeames?

William Makepeace Thackeray
(1811–1863)

DAME TROTTYPEG

In London-town Dame Trottypeg
    Lived high up in a garret;
And with her lived a wee pet Dog,
    A Tom-cat and a Parrot.

A cleverer or a funnier dog
    I'm sure you never saw;
For, like a sailor, he could dance
    A hornpipe on one paw.

And all the while the doggie danced,
    That Pussy-cat was able
Just like a flute to play his tail
    Upon the kitchen table.

TWO NICE DOGS

Two little Dogs went out for a walk,
    And it was windy weather,
So for fear the wind should blow them away,
    They tied their tails together.

They tied their tails with a yard of tape,
    And the wind it blew and blew,
As sharp and keen as a carving-knife,
    And cut the tape in two.

And away and away, like kites, in the air
    Those two little Dogs flew about,
Till one little Dog was blown to bits,
    And the other turn'd inside out.

VERY POORLY

Two Cats sat on a garden-wall,
    For an hour or so together;
At first they talked about nothing at all,
    And then they talked of the weather.

The little Pussy-cat, afraid of the cold,
    Had a wrapper to wrap her chin in;
But the big Pussy-cat, more silly than that,
    Kept her tail in a bag of linen.

Said the little Pussy-cat to the big Pussy-cat,
    "You've not very much to ail of";
And so angry at that was the big Pussy-cat,
    That she bit the little one's tail off.

IF

How odd it would be if all the Cows
Were to run up all the trees,
And the Cats were to eat up all the Mice,
And the mice eat all the cheese.

D'Arcy W. Thompson (1829–1902)
Illustrations by Charles H. Bennett (1829–1867)

Dame Wiggins of Lee
Was a worthy old soul,
As e'er threaded a needle,
Or wash'd in a bowl:
She held mice and rats
In such antipathy;
That seven fine cats
Kept Dame Wiggins of Lee.

The rats and mice scared
By this fierce whisker'd crew,
The poor seven cats
Soon had nothing to do;
So, as any one idle
She ne'er loved to see,
She sent them to school,
Did Dame Wiggins of Lee.

The Master soon wrote
That they all of them knew
How to read the word "milk"
And to spell the word "mew."
And they all washed their faces
Before they took tea:
"Were there ever such dears!"
Said Dame Wiggins of Lee.

He had also thought well
To comply with their wish
To spend all their play-time
In learning to fish
For stitlings; they sent her
A present of three,
Which, fried, were a feast
For Dame Wiggins of Lee.

But soon she grew tired
Of living alone;
So she sent for her cats
From school to come home.
Each rowing a wherry,
Returning you see:
The frolic made merry
Dame Wiggins of Lee.

The Dame was quite pleas'd,
And ran out to market;
When she came back
They were mending the carpet.
The needle each handled
As brisk as a bee;
"Well done, my good cats,"
Said Dame Wiggins of Lee.

Engravings by W. H. Hooper
Drawings by Kate Greenaway (1846–1901)

When spring-time came back
They had breakfast of curds;
And were greatly afraid
Of disturbing the birds.
"If you sit, like good cats,
All the seven in a tree,
They will teach you to sing!"
Said Dame Wiggins of Lee.

So they sat in a tree,
And said "Beautiful! Hark!"
And they listened and looked
In the clouds for the lark.
Then sang, by the fireside,
Symphoniously,
A song without words
To Dame Wiggins of Lee.

Richard Scrafton Sharpe
Additional verses by John Ruskin (1819–1900)

THE OWL AND THE PUSSY-CAT

I

The Owl and the Pussy-Cat went to sea
    In a beautiful pea-green boat,
They took some honey, and plenty of money,
    Wrapped up in a five-pound note.
The Owl looked up to the stars above,
    And sang to a small guitar,
"O lovely Pussy! O Pussy, my love,
    What a beautiful Pussy you are,
        You are,
        You are!
What a beautiful Pussy you are!"

II

Pussy said to the Owl, "You elegant fowl!
    How charmingly sweet you sing!
O let us be married! too long we have tarried:
    But what shall we do for a ring?"
They sailed away for a year and a day,
    To the land where the Bong-tree grows,
And there in a wood a Piggy-wig stood,
    With a ring at the end of his nose,
        His nose,
        His nose,
With a ring at the end of his nose.

III

"Dear Pig, are you willing to sell for one shilling
    Your ring?" Said the Piggy, "I will."
So they took it away, and were married next day
    By the Turkey who lives on the hill.
They dined on mince, and slices of quince,
    Which they ate with a runcible spoon;
And hand in hand, on the edge of the sand,
    They danced by the light of the moon,
        The moon,
        The moon,
They danced by the light of the moon.

Edward Lear (1812–1888)
Illustrations by L. Leslie Brooke (1862–1940)

THE CAPTAIN.
Illustration by Walter Crane (1845–1915)

SONNET TO VAUXHALL

"The English Garden."—Mason

The cold transparent ham is on my fork—
    It hardly rains—and hark the bell!—ding-dingle—
Away! Three thousand feet at gravel work,
    Mocking a Vauxhall shower!—Married and Single
Crush—rush;—Soak'd Silks with wet white Satin mingle.
    Hengler! Madame! round whom all bright sparks lurk,
Calls audibly on Mr. and Mrs. Pringle
    To study the Sublime, &c.—(vide Burke)
All Noses are upturn'd!—Whish-ish!—On high
    The rocket rushes—trails—just steals in sight—
Then droops and melts in bubbles of blue light—
    And Darkness reigns—Then balls flare up and die—
Wheels whiz—smack crackers—serpents twist—and then
    Back to the cold transparent ham again!

Thomas Hood (1799–1845)

OLD VAUXHALL GARDENS. *Pen, ink, and watercolor drawing by Thomas Rowlandson (1756–1827)*

Courtesy Victoria and Albert Museum

INCIDENTS IN THE LIFE
OF MY UNCLE ARLY

I

O my aged Uncle Arly!
Sitting on a heap of Barley
    Thro' the silent hours of night, —
Close beside a leafy thicket: —
On his nose there was a Cricket, —
In his hat a Railway-Ticket
    (But his shoes were far too tight).

II

Long ago, in youth, he squander'd
All his goods away, and wander'd
    To the Tiniskoop-hills afar.
There on golden sunsets blazing,
Every evening found him gazing, —
Singing, — "Orb! you're quite amazing!
    How I wonder what you are!"

III

Like the ancient Medes and Persians,
Always by his own exertions
    He subsisted on those hills; —
Whiles, —by teaching children spelling, —
Or at times by merely yelling, —
Or at intervals by selling
    "Propter's Nicodemus Pills."

IV

Later, in his morning rambles
He perceived the moving brambles —
    Something square and white disclose; —
'Twas a First-class Railway-Ticket;
But, on stooping down to pick it
Off the ground, —a pea-green Cricket
    Settled on my uncle's Nose.

V

Never—never more, —oh! never,
Did that Cricket leave him ever, —
    Dawn or evening, day or night; —
Clinging as a constant treasure, —
Chirping with a cheerious measure, —
Wholly to my uncle's pleasure
    (Though his shoes were far too tight).

VI

So for three and forty winters,
Till his shoes were worn to splinters,
    All those hills he wander'd o'er, —
Sometimes silent; —sometimes yelling; —
Till he came to Borley-Melling,
Near his old ancestral dwelling
    (But his shoes were far too tight).

VII

On a little heap of Barley
Died my agèd Uncle Arly,
    And they buried him one night; —
Close beside the leafy thicket; —
There, —his hat and Railway-Ticket; —
There, —his ever-faithful Cricket
    (But his shoes were far too tight).

Edward Lear (1812–1888)
Illustration by L. Leslie Brooke (1862–1940)

THE CUMMERBUND

An Indian Poem

I

She sat upon her Dobie,
　　To watch the Evening Star,
And all the Punkahs as they passed
　　Cried, "My! how fair you are!"
Around her bower, with quivering leaves,
　　The tall Kamsamahs grew,
And Kitmutgars in wild festoons
　　Hung down from Tchokis blue.

II

Below her home the river rolled
　　With soft meloobious sound,
Where golden-finned Chuprassies swam,
　　In myriads circling round.
Above, on tallest trees remote,
　　Green Ayahs perched alone,
And all night long the Mussak moaned
　　Its melancholy tone.

III

And where the purple Nullahs threw
    Their branches far and wide,
And silvery Goreewallahs flew
    In silence, side by side,
The little Bheesties' twittering cry
    Rose on the fragrant air,
And oft the angry Jampan howled
    Deep in his hateful lair.

IV

She sat upon her Dobie, —
    She heard the Nimmak hum, —
When all at once a cry arose:
    "The Cummerbund is come!"
In vain she fled; —with open jaws
    The angry monster followed,
And so (before assistance came),
    That Lady Fair was swallowed.

V

They sought in vain for even a bone
    Respectfully to bury;
They said, "Hers was a dreadful fate!"
    (And Echo answered, "Very.")
They nailed her Dobie to the wall,
    Where last her form was seen,
And underneath they wrote these words,
    In yellow, blue, and green: —
"Beware, ye Fair! Ye Fair, beware!
    Nor sit out late at night,
Lest horrid Cummerbunds should come,
    And swallow you outright."

Edward Lear (1812–1888)
Illustration by L. Leslie Brooke (1862–1940)

CALICO PIE

I

Calico Pie,
The little Birds fly
Down to the calico tree,
Their wings were blue,
And they sang "Tilly-loo!"
Till away they flew—
And they never came back to me!
They never came back!
They never came back!
They never came back to me!

II

Calico Jam,
The little Fish swam
Over the syllabub sea,
He took off his hat,
To the Sole and the Sprat,
And the Willeby-wat—
But he never came back to me!
He never came back!
He never came back!
He never came back to me!

III

Calico Ban,
    The little Mice ran,
To be ready in time for tea,
    Flippity flup,
    They drank it all up,
    And danced in the cup—
But they never came back to me!
    They never came back!
    They never came back!
They never came back to me!

IV

Calico Drum,
    The Grasshoppers come,
The Butterfly, Beetle, and Bee,
    Over the ground,
    Around and round,
    With a hop and a bound—
But they never came back!
    They never came back!
    They never came back!
They never came back to me!

Edward Lear (1812–1888)

59

LINES TO A YOUNG LADY

"How pleasant to know Mr. Lear!"
    Who has written such volumes of stuff!
Some think him ill-tempered and queer,
    But a few think him pleasant enough.

His mind is concrete and fastidious,
    His nose is remarkably big;
His visage is more or less hideous,
    His beard it resembles a wig.

He has ears, and two eyes, and ten fingers,
    Leastways if you reckon two thumbs;
Long ago he was one of the singers,
    But now he is one of the dumbs.

He sits in a beautiful parlour,
    With hundreds of books on the wall;
He drinks a great deal of Marsala,
    But never gets tipsy at all.

He has many friends, laymen and clerical,
    Old Foss is the name of his cat;
His body is perfectly spherical,
    He weareth a runcible hat.

When he walks in a waterproof white,
    The children run after him so!
Calling out, "He's come out in his night-
    gown, that crazy old Englishman, oh!"

He weeps by the side of the ocean,
    He weeps on the top of the hill;
He purchases pancakes and lotion,
    And chocolate shrimps from the mill.

He reads but he cannot speak Spanish,
    He cannot abide ginger-beer:
Ere the days of his pilgrimage vanish,
    How pleasant to know Mr. Lear!

Edward Lear (1812–1888)

VERSES

When fishes set umbrellas up
    If the rain-drops run,
Lizards will want their parasols
    To shade them from the sun.

The peacock has a score of eyes,
    With which he cannot see;
The cod-fish has a silent sound,
    However that may be.

No dandelions tell the time,
    Although they turn to clocks;
Cat's cradle does not hold the cat,
    Nor foxglove fit the fox.

Christina Georgina Rossetti (1830–1894)
Illustration by Arthur Hughes

LOVERS AND A REFLECTION

In moss-prankt dells which the sunbeams flatter
    (And heaven it knoweth what that may mean;
Meaning, however, is no great matter)
    Where woods are a-tremble with words a-tween;

Thro' God's own heather we wonned together,
    I and my Willie (O love my love):
I need hardly remark it was glorious weather,
    And flitter-bats wavered alow, above:

Boats were curtseying, rising, bowing,
    (Boats in that climate are so polite,)
And sands were a ribbon of green endowing,
    And O the sun-dazzle on bark and bight!

Thro' the rare red heather we danced together
    (O love my Willie) and smelt for flowers:
I must mention again it was glorious weather,
    Rhymes are so scarce in this world of ours:

By rises that flushed with their purple favors,
    Thro' becks that brattled o'er grasses sheen,
We walked or waded, we two young shavers,
    Thanking our stars we were both so green.

We journeyed in parallels, I and Willie,
    In fortunate parallels! Butterflies,
Hid in weltering shadows of daffodilly
    Or marjoram, kept making peacock eyes:

Song-birds darted about, some inky
    As coal, some snowy (I ween) as curds;
Or rosy as pinks, or as roses pinky—
    They reek of no eerie To-come, those birds!

But they skim over bents which the mill-stream washes,
    Or hang in the lift 'neath a white cloud's hem;
They need no parasols, no goloshes;
    And good Mrs. Trimmer she feedeth them.

Then we thrid God's cowslips (as erst his heather),
      That endowed the wan grass with their golden blooms;
And snapt—(it was perfectly charming weather)—
      Our fingers at Fate and her goddess-glooms:

And Willie 'gan sing—(Oh, his notes were fluty;
      Wafts fluttered them out to the white-winged sea)—
Something made up of rhymes that have done much duty,
      Rhymes (better to put it) of "ancientry":

Bowers of flowers encountered showers
      In William's carol—(O love my Willie!)
Then he bade sorrow borrow from blithe tomorrow
      I quite forget what—say a daffodilly.

A nest in a hollow, "with buds to follow,"
      I think occurred next in his nimble strain;
And clay that was "kneaden" of course in Eden—
      A rhyme most novel I do maintain:

Mists, bones, the singer himself, love-stories,
      And all least furlable things got furled;
Not with any design to conceal their glories,
      But simply and solely to rhyme with world.

O if billows and pillows and hours and flowers,
      And all the brave rhymes of an elder day,
Could be furled together, this genial weather,
      And carted or carried on wafts away,
Nor ever again trotted out—ah me!
How much fewer volumes of verse there'd be.

Charles Stuart Calverly (1831–1884)

JABBERWOCKY

'Twas brillig, and the slithy toves
    Did gyre and gimble in the wabe;
All mimsy were the borogoves,
    And the mome raths outgrabe.

"Beware the Jabberwock, my son!
    The jaws that bite, the claws that catch!
Beware the Jubjub bird, and shun
    The frumious Bandersnatch!"

He took his vorpal sword in hand:
    Long time the manxome foe he sought.
So rested he by the Tumtum tree,
    And stood awhile in thought.

And as in uffish thought he stood,
    The Jabberwock with eyes of flame,
Came whiffling through the tulgey wood,
    And burbled as it came!

One, two! One, two! And through, and through
    The vorpal blade went snicker-snack!
He left it dead, and with its head
    He went galumphing back.

"And hast thou slain the Jabberwock?
    Come to my arms, my beamish boy!
Oh, frabjous day! Callooh! callay!"
    He chortled in his joy.

'Twas brillig, and the slithy toves
    Did gyre and gimble in the wabe;
All mimsy were the borogoves
    And the mome raths outgrabe.

Lewis Carroll (1832–1898)
Illustration by John Tenniel (1820–1914)

THE WALRUS AND THE CARPENTER

The Walrus and the Carpenter
    Were walking close at hand;
They wept like anything to see
    Such quantities of sand:
"If this were only cleared away,"
    They said, "it would be grand!"

    . . . . .

"The time has come," the Walrus said,
    "To talk of many things:
Of shoes—and ships—and sealing-wax—
    Of cabbages—and kings—
And why the sea is boiling hot—
    And whether pigs have wings."

"But, wait a bit," the Oysters cried,
    "Before we have our chat;
For some of us are out of breath,
    And all of us are fat!"
"No hurry!" said the Carpenter.
    They thanked him much for that.

"A loaf of bread," the Walrus said,
    "Is what we chiefly need:
Pepper and vinegar besides
    Are very good indeed—
Now if you're ready, Oysters dear,
    We can begin to feed."

"But not on us!" the Oysters cried,
      Turning a little blue.
"After such kindness, that would be
      A dismal thing to do!"
"The night is fine," the Walrus said.
      "Do you admire the view?

"It was so kind of you to come!
      And you are very nice!"
The Carpenter said nothing but
      "Cut us another slice:
I wish you were not quite so deaf—
      I've had to ask you twice!"

"It seems a shame," the Walrus said,
      "To play them such a trick,
After we've brought them out so far,
      And made them trot so quick!"
The Carpenter said nothing but
      "The butter's spread too thick!"

"I weep for you," the Walrus said:
      "I deeply sympathize."
With sobs and tears he sorted out
      Those of the largest size
Holding his pocket-handkerchief
      Before his streaming eyes.

"O Oysters," said the Carpenter,
      "You've had a pleasant run!
Shall we be trotting home again?"
      But answer came there none—
And this was scarcely odd, because
      They'd eaten every one.

Lewis Carroll (1832–1898)
Illustrations by John Tenniel (1820–1914)

A FROG HE WOULD
A-WOOING GO

A frog he would a-wooing go,
    Heigho, says Rowley!
Whether his mother would let him or no.
    With a rowley-powley, gammon and spinach,
    Heigho, says Anthony Rowley!

So off he set with his opera hat,
    Heigho, says Rowley!
And on his way he met with a Rat
    With a rowley-powley, gammon and spinach,
    Heigho, says Anthony Rowley!

"Pray, Mr. Rat, will you go with me,"
    Heigho, says Rowley!
"Pretty Miss Mousey for to see?"
    With a rowley-powley, gammon and spinach,
    Heigho, says Anthony Rowley!

Now soon they arrived at Mousey's Hall,
    Heigho, says Rowley!
And gave a loud knock, and gave a loud call.
    With a rowley-powley, gammon and spinach,
    Heigho, says Anthony Rowley!

"Pray, Miss Mousey, are you within?"
　　Heigho, says Rowley!
"Oh, yes, kind Sirs, I'm sitting to spin."
　　With a rowley-powley, gammon and spinach,
　　Heigho, says Anthony Rowley!

"Pray, Miss Mouse, will you give us some beer?"
　　Heigho, says Rowley!
"For Froggy and I are fond of good cheer."
　　With a rowley-powley, gammon and spinach,
　　Heigho, says Anthony Rowley!

"Pray, Mr. Frog, will you give us a song?"
　　Heigho, says Rowley!
"But let it be something that's not very long."
　　With a rowley-powley, gammon and spinach,
　　Heigho, says Anthony Rowley!

69

"Indeed, Miss Mouse," replied Mr. Frog,
    Heigho, says Rowley!
"A cold has made me as hoarse as a Hog."
        With a rowley-powley, gammon and spinach,
        Heigho, says Anthony Rowley!

"Since you have caught cold," Miss Mousey said,
    Heigho, says Rowley!
"I'll sing you a song that I have just made."
        With a rowley-powley, gammon and spinach,
        Heigho, says Anthony Rowley!

But while they were all thus a merry-making,
    Heigho, says Rowley!
A cat and her kittens came tumbling in.
        With a rowley-powley, gammon and spinach,
        Heigho, says Anthony Rowley!

The cat she seized the rat by the crown;
    Heigho, says Rowley!
The kittens they pulled the little mouse down.
    With a rowley-powley, gammon and spinach,
    Heigho, says Anthony Rowley!

This put Mr. Frog in a terrible fright;
    Heigho, says Rowley!
He took up his hat, and he wished them good night.
    With a rowley-powley, gammon and spinach,
    Heigho, says Anthony Rowley!

But as Froggy was crossing a silvery brook,
    Heigho, says Rowley!
A lily-white duck came and gobbled him up.
    With a rowley-powley, gammon and spinach,
    Heigho, says Anthony Rowley!

So there was an end of one, two, and three,
    Heigho, says Rowley!
The rat, the mouse, and the little frog-gee!
    With a rowley-powley, gammon and spinach,
    Heigho, says Anthony Rowley!

Anonymous

Illustrations by Randolph Caldecott (1846–1886)

"YOU ARE OLD, FATHER WILLIAM"

"You are old, Father William," the young man said,
    "And your hair has become very white;
And yet you incessantly stand on your head—
    Do you think, at your age, it is right?"

"In my youth," Father William replied to his son,
    "I feared it might injure the brain;
But, now that I'm perfectly sure I have none.
    Why, I do it again and again."

"You are old," said the youth, "as I mentioned before,
    And have grown most uncommonly fat;
Yet you turned a back-somersault in at the door—
    Pray, what is the reason of that?"

"In my youth," said the sage, as he shook his grey locks,
    "I kept all my limbs very supple
By the use of this ointment—one shilling the box—
    Allow me to sell you a couple?"

"You are old," said the youth, "and your jaws are too weak
    For anything tougher than suet;
Yet you finished the goose, with the bones and the beak—
    Pray how did you manage to do it?"

"In my youth," said his father, "I took to the law,
    And argued each case with my wife;
And the muscular strength, which it gave to my jaw,
    Has lasted the rest of my life."

"You are old," said the youth, "one would hardly suppose
    That your eye was as steady as ever;
Yet you balanced an eel on the end of your nose—
    What made you so awfully clever?"

"I have answered three questions, and that is enough,"
    Said his father; "don't give yourself airs!
Do you think I can listen all day to such stuff?
    Be off, or I'll kick you down stairs!"

Lewis Carroll (1832–1898)
Illustrations by John Tenniel (1820–1914)

THE MAD GARDENER'S SONG

He thought he saw an Elephant,
    That practised on a fife:
He looked again, and found it was
    A letter from his wife.
"At length I realize," he said,
    "The bitterness of Life!"

He thought he saw a Buffalo
    Upon the chimney-piece:
He looked again, and found it was
    His Sister's Husband's Niece.
"Unless you leave this house," he said,
    "I'll send for the Police!"

He thought he saw a Rattlesnake
    That questioned him in Greek:
He looked again, and found it was
    The Middle of Next Week.
"The one thing I regret," he said,
    "Is that it cannot speak!"

He thought he saw a Banker's Clerk
    Descending from the bus:
He looked again, and found it was
    A Hippopotamus:
"If this should stay to dine," he said,
    "There won't be much for us!"

He thought he saw a Kangaroo
    That worked a coffee-mill:
He looked again, and found it was
    A Vegetable-Pill.
"Were I to swallow this," he said,
    "I should be very ill!"

He thought he saw a Coach-and-Four
    That stood beside his bed:
He looked again, and found it was
    A Bear without a Head.
"Poor thing," he said, "poor silly thing!
    It's waiting to be fed!"

He thought he saw an Albatross
    That fluttered round the lamp:
He looked again, and found it was
    A Penny-Postage-Stamp.
"You'd best be getting home," he said:
    "The nights are very damp!"

He thought he saw a Garden-Door
    That opened with a key:
He looked again, and found it was
    A Double Rule of Three:
"And all its mystery," he said,
    "Is clear as day to me!"

He thought he saw an Argument
    That proved he was the Pope:
He looked again, and found it was
    A Bar of Mottled Soap.
"A fact so dread," he faintly said,
    "Extinguishes all hope!"

Lewis Carroll (1832–1898)
Illustrations by Harry Furniss (1854–1925)

THE HUNTING OF THE SNARK
Fit the Fourth

· · · · ·

" 'Tis a pitiful tale," said the Bellman, whose face
    Had grown longer at every word;
"But, now that you've stated the whole of your case,
    More debate would be simply absurd.

"The rest of my speech" (he explained to his men)
    "You shall hear when I've leisure to speak it.
But the Snark is at hand, let me tell you again!
    'Tis your glorious duty to seek it!

"To seek it with thimbles, to seek it with care;
    To pursue it with forks and hope;
To threaten its life with a railway-share;
    To charm it with smiles and soap!

"For the Snark's a peculiar creature, that won't
    Be caught in a commonplace way.
Do all that you know, and try all that you don't:
    Not a chance must be wasted to-day!

"For England expects—I forebear to proceed:
    'Tis a maxim tremendous, but trite:
And you'd best be unpacking the things that you need
    To rig yourselves out for the fight."

· · · · ·

"TO PURSUE IT WITH FORKS AND HOPE . . ."

THE BEAVER BROUGHT PAPER, PORTFOLIO, PENS.

Fit the Fifth

• • • • •

"The thing can be done," said the Butcher, "I think.
    The thing must be done, I am sure.
The thing shall be done! Bring me paper and ink,
    The best there is time to procure."

The Beaver brought paper, portfolio, pens,
    And ink in unfailing supplies:
While strange creepy creatures came out of their dens,
    And watched them with wondering eyes.

So engrossed was the Butcher, he heeded them not,
    As he wrote with a pen in each hand,
And explained all the while in a popular style
    Which the Beaver could well understand.

"Taking Three as the subject to reason about—
    A convenient number to state—
We add Seven, and Ten, and then multiply out
    By One Thousand diminished by Eight.

"The result we proceed to divide, as you see,
    By Nine Hundred and Ninety and Two:
Then subtract Seventeen, and the answer must be
    Exactly and perfectly true.

• • • • •

Lewis Carroll (1832–1898)
Illustrations by Henry Holiday (1839–1927)

LITTLE BIRDS

Little Birds are dining
    Warily and well
      Hid in mossy cell:
Hid, I say, by waiters
Gorgeous in their gaiters—
      I've a tale to tell.

Little Birds are seeking
    Hecatombs of haws,
      Dressed in snowy gauze:
Dressed, I say, in fringes
Half alive with hinges—
      Thus they break the laws.

Little Birds are feeding
    Justices with jam,
      Rich with frizzled ham:
Rich, I say, in oysters
Haunting shady cloisters—
      That is what I am.

Little Birds are teaching
    Tigresses to smile,
      Innocent of guile:
Smile, I say, not smirkle—
Mouth a semicircle,
      That's the proper style!

Little Birds are sleeping
    All among the pins,
      Where the loser wins:
Where, I say, he sneezes,
When and how he pleases—
      So the Tale begins.

Little Birds are writing
    Interesting books,
      To be read by cooks:
Read, I say, not roasted—
Letterpress, when toasted,
      Loses its good looks.

Little Birds are playing
    Bagpipes on the shore,
      Where the tourists snore:
"Thanks!" they cry. " 'Tis thrilling
Take, oh, take this shilling!
      Let us have no more."

Little Birds are bathing
    Crocodiles in cream,
      Like a happy dream:
Like, but not so lasting—
Crocodiles, when fasting,
      Are not all they seem!

Little Birds are choking
    Baronets with bun,
      Taught to fire a gun:
Taught, I say, to splinter
Salmon in the winter—
      Merely for the fun.

Little Birds are hiding
    Crimes in carpet-bags,
      Blessed by happy stags:
Blessed, I say, though beaten—
Since our friends are eaten
      When the memory flags.

Little Birds are tasting
    Gratitude and gold,
      Pale with sudden cold:
Pale, I say, and wrinkled—
When the bells have tinkled,
      And the Tale is told.

Lewis Carroll (1832–1898)
Illustrations by Harry Furniss (1854–1925)
as engraved by Joseph Swain

THE KING-FISHER SONG

King Fisher courted Lady Bird—
Sing Beans, sing Bones, sing Butterflies!
    "Find me my match," he said,
    "With such a noble head—
With such a beard, as white as curd—
    With such expressive eyes!"

"Yet pins have heads," said Lady Bird—
Sing Prunes, sing Prawns, sing Primrose-Hill!
    "And, where you stick them in,
    They stay, and thus a pin
Is very much to be preferred
    To one that's never still!"

"Oysters have beards," said Lady Bird—
Sing Flies, sing Frogs, sing Fiddle-strings!
    "I love them, for I know
    They never chatter so:
They would not say one single word—
    Not if you crowned them Kings!"

"Needles have eyes," said Lady Bird—
Sing Cats, sing Corks, sing Cowslip-tea!
    "And they are sharp—just what
    Your Majesty is *not*:
So get you gone—'tis too absurd
    To come a-courting *me!*"

Lewis Carroll (1832–1898)
Illustration by Harry Furniss (1854–1925)

THE MONKEY'S GLUE

When the monkey in his madness
    Took the glue to mend his voice,
'Twas the crawfish showed his sadness
    That the bluebird could rejoice.

Then the perspicacious parrot
    Sought to save the suicide
By administering carrot,
    But the monkey merely died.

So the crawfish and the parrot
    Sauntered slowly toward the sea,
While the bluebird stole the carrot
    And returned the glue to me.

Goldwin Goldsmith

LIMERICK

Un marin naufragé (de Doncastre)
Pour prière, au milieu du désastre
    Répétait à genoux
    Ces mots simples et doux: —
"Scintillez, scintillez, petit astre!"

George du Maurier (1834–1896)

LIMERICK

There was a young man who was bitten
By twenty-two cats and a kitten;
    Sighed he, "It is clear
    My finish is near;
No matter; I'll die like a Briton!"

Walter Parke

SWISS AIR

I'm a gay tra, la, la,
    With my fal, lal, la, la,
    And my bright—
And my light—
    Tra, la, le.

        [Repeat]

Then laugh, ha, ha, ha,
And ring, ting, ling, ling,
And sing, fal, la, la,
    La la, le.

        [Repeat]

Bret Harte (1836–1902)

AT A READING

The spare Professor, grave and bald,
Began his paper. It was called,
I think, "A brief Historic Glance
At Russia, Germany, and France."
A glance, but to my best belief
'Twas almost anything but brief—
A wide survey, in which the earth
Was seen before mankind had birth;
Strange monsters basked them in the sun,
Behemoth, armored glyptodon,
And in the dawn's unpractised ray
The transient dodo winged its way;
Then, by degrees, through silt and slough,
We reached Berlin—I don't know how.
The good Professor's monotone
Had turned me into senseless stone
Instanter, but that near me sat
Hypatia in her new spring hat,
Blue-eyed, intent, with lips whose bloom
Lighted the heavy-curtained room.
Hypatia—ah, what lovely things

Are fashioned out of eighteen springs!
At first, in sums of this amount,
The blighting winters do not count.
Just as my eyes were growing dim
With heaviness, I saw that slim,
Erect, elastic figure there,
Like a pond-lily taking air.
She looked so fresh, so wise, so neat,
So altogether crisp and sweet,
I quite forgot what Bismarck said,
And why the Emperor shook his head,
And how it was Von Moltke's frown
Cost France another frontier town.
The only facts I took away
From the Professor's theme that day
Were these: a forehead broad and low,
Such as the antique sculptures show;
A chin to Greek perfection true;
Eyes of Astarte's tender blue;
A high complexion without fleck
Or flaw, and curls about her neck.

Bret Harte (1836–1902)

AN UNSUSPECTED FACT

If down his throat a man should choose
In fun, to jump or slide,
He'd scrape his shoes against his teeth,
Nor dirt his own inside.
But if his teeth were lost and gone,
And not a stump to scrape upon,
He'd see at once how very pat
His tongue lay there by way of mat,
And he would wipe his feet on *that!*

Edward Cannon

GENERAL JOHN

The bravest names for fire and flames,
    And all that mortal durst,
Were General John and Private James,
    Of the Sixty-seventy-first.

General John was a soldier tried,
    A chief of warlike dons;
A haughty stride and a withering pride
    Were Major-General John.

A sneer would play on his martial phiz,
    Superior birth to show;
"Pish!" was a favorite word of his,
    And he often said "Ho! ho!"

Full-Private James described might be,
    As a man of mournful mind;
No characteristic trait had he
    Of any distinctive kind.

From the ranks, one day, cried Private James,
    "Oh! Major-General John,
I've doubts of our respective names,
    My mournful mind upon.

"A glimmering thought occurs to me,
    (Its source I can't unearth),
But I've a kind of notion we
    Were cruelly changed at birth.

"I've a strange idea, each other's names
    That we have each got on.
Such things have been," said Private James.
    "They have!" sneered General John.

"My General John, I swear upon
    My oath I think it is so—"
"Pish!" proudly sneered his General John,
    And he also said "Ho! ho!"

"My General John! my General John!
    My General John!" quoth he,
"This aristocratical sneer upon
    Your face I blush to see.

"No truly great or generous cove
    Deserving of them names
Would sneer at a fixed idea that's drove
    In the mind of a Private James!"

Said General John, "Upon your claims
    No need your breath to waste;
If this is a joke, Full-Private James,
    It's a joke of doubtful taste.

"But being a man of doubtless worth,
    If you feel certain quite
That we were probably changed at birth,
    I'll venture to say you're right."

So General John as Private James
    Fell in, parade upon;
And Private James, by change of names,
    Was Major-General John.

W. S. Gilbert (1836–1911)
Engraving by "Bab" (W. S. Gilbert)

HYDER IDDLE

Hyder iddle diddle dell,
    A yard of pudding is not an ell,
Not forgetting tweedle-dye,
    A tailor's goose will never fly.

Anonymous

OFF TO WAR.
Grandville (1803–1847)

THE STORY OF THE MAN THAT
WENT OUT SHOOTING

This is the man that shoots the hares;
This is the coat he always wears:
With game-bag, powder-horn and gun
He's going out to have some fun.
The hare sits snug in leaves and grass,
And laughs to see the green man pass.
He finds it hard, without a pair
Of spectacles, to shoot the hare.

Now, as the sun grew very hot,
And he a heavy gun had got,
He lay down underneath a tree
And went to sleep, as you may see.
And, while he slept like any top,
The little hare came, hop, hop, hop,
Took gun and spectacles, and then
On her hind legs went off again.

The green man wakes and sees her place
The spectacles upon her face;
And now she's trying all she can,
To shoot the sleepy, green-coat man.
He cries and screams and runs away;
The hare runs after him all day
And hears him call out everywhere:
"Help! Fire! Help! The Hare! The Hare!"

At last he stumbled at the well
Head over ears, and in he fell.
The hare stopp'd short, took aim, and hark!
Bang went the gun, — she miss'd her mark!

The poor man's wife was drinking up
Her coffee in her coffee-cup;
The gun shot cup and saucer through;
"O dear!" cried she, "what shall I do?"
There liv'd close by the cottage there
The hare's own child, the little hare;
And while she stood upon her toes,
The coffee fell and burn'd her nose.
"O dear!" she cried, with spoon in hand,
"Such fun I do not understand."

    Dr. Heinrich Hoffmann (1809–1894)

DARWINITY

Power to thine elbow, thou newest of sciences,
    All the old landmarks are ripe for decay;
Wars are but shadows, and so are alliances,
    Darwin the great is the man of the day.

All other 'ologies want an apology;
    Bread's a mistake—Science offers a stone;
Nothing is true but Anthropobiology—
    Darwin the great understands it alone.

Mighty the great evolutionist teacher is,
    Licking Morphology clean into shape;
Lord! what an ape the Professor or Preacher is,
    Ever to doubt his descent from an ape.

Man's an Anthropoid—he cannot help that, you know—
    First evoluted from Pongos of old;
He's but a branch of the *catarrhine* cat, you know—
    Monkey I mean— that's an ape with a cold.

Fast dying out are man's later Appearances,
    Cataclysmitic Geologies gone;
Now of Creation completed the clearance is,
    Darwin alone you must anchor upon.

Primitive Life—Organisms were chemical,
    Bursting spontaneous under the sea;
Purely subaqueous, panaquademical,
    Was the original Crystal of Me.

I'm the Apostle of mighty Darwinity,
    Stands for Divinity—sounds much the same—
Apo-theistico-Pan-Asininity
    Only can doubt whence the lot of us came.

Down on your knees, Superstition and Flunkeydom!
    Won't you accept such plain doctrines instead?
What is so simple as primitive Monkeydom
    Born in the sea with a cold in its head?

Herman Merivale (1839–1906)

GENTLE ALICE BROWN

It was a robber's daughter, and her name was Alice Brown.
Her father was the terror of a small Italian town;
Her mother was a foolish, weak, but amiable old thing;
But it isn't of her parents that I'm going for to sing.

As Alice was a-sitting at her window-sill one day,
A beautiful young gentleman he chanced to pass that way;
She cast her eyes upon him, and he looked so good and true,
That she thought, "I could be happy with a gentleman like you!"

And every morning passed her house that cream of gentlemen,
She knew she might expect him at a quarter unto ten,
A sorter in the Custom-house, it was his daily road
(The Custom-house was fifteen minutes' walk from her abode).

But Alice was a pious girl, who knew it wasn't wise
To look at strange young sorters with expressive purple eyes;
So she sought the village priest to whom her family confessed,
The priest by whom their little sins were carefully assessed.

"Oh, holy father," Alice said, " 't would grieve you, would it not?
To discover that I was a most disreputable lot!
Of all unhappy sinners I'm the most unhappy one!"
The padre said, "Whatever have you been and gone and done?"

"I have helped mamma to steal a little kiddy from its dad,
I've assisted dear papa in cutting up a little lad.
I've planned a little burglary and forged a little check,
And slain a little baby for the coral on its neck!"

The worthy pastor heaved a sigh, and dropped a silent tear—
And said, "You mustn't judge yourself too heavily, my dear—
It's wrong to murder babies, little corals for to fleece;
But sins like these one expiates at half-a-crown apiece.

"Girls will be girls—you're very young, and flighty in your mind;
Old heads upon young shoulders we must not expect to find:
We mustn't be too hard upon these little girlish tricks—
Let's see—five crimes at half-a-crown—exactly twelve-and-six."

"Oh, father," little Alice cried, "your kindness makes me weep,
You do these little things for me so singularly cheap—
Your thoughtful liberality I never can forget;
But O there is another crime I haven't mentioned yet!

"A pleasant-looking gentleman, with pretty purple eyes,
I've noticed at my window, as I've sat a-catching flies;
He passes by it every day as certain as can be—
I blush to say I've winked at him and he has winked at me!"

"For shame," said Father Paul, "my erring daughter! On my word
This is the most distressing news that I have ever heard.
Why, naughty girl, your excellent papa has pledged your hand
To a promising young robber, the lieutenant of his band!

"This dreadful piece of news will pain your worthy parents so!
They are the most remunerative customers I know;
For many many years they've kept starvation from my doors,
I never knew so criminal a family as yours!

"The common country folk in this insipid neighborhood
Have nothing to confess, they're so ridiculously good;
And if you marry any one respectable at all,
Why, you'll reform, and what will then become of Father Paul?"

The worthy priest, he up and drew his cowl upon his crown,
And started off in haste to tell the news to Robber Brown;
To tell him how his daughter, who now was for marriage fit,
Had winked upon a sorter, who reciprocated it.

Good Robber Brown, he muffled up his anger pretty well,
He said, "I have a notion, and that notion I will tell;
I will nab this gay young sorter, terrify him into fits,
And get my gentle wife to chop him into little bits.

"I've studied human nature, and I know a thing or two,
Though a girl may fondly love a living gent, as many do—
A feeling of disgust upon her senses there will fall
When she looks upon his body chopped particularly small."

He traced that gallant sorter to a still suburban square;
He watched his opportunity and seized him unaware;
He took a life-preserver and he hit him on the head,
And Mrs. Brown dissected him before she went to bed.

And pretty little Alice grew more settled in her mind,
She nevermore was guilty of a weakness of the kind,
Until at length good Robber Brown bestowed her pretty hand
On the promising young robber, the lieutenant of his band.

W. S. Gilbert (1836–1911)
Illustration by "Bab" (W. S. Gilbert)

A MAIDEN THERE LIVED

A maiden there lived in a large market-town,
Whose skin was much fairer—than any that's brown—
Her eyes were as dark as the coals in the mine,
And when they weren't shut, why they always would shine.
 With a black eye, blue eye, blear eye, pig's eye, swivel eye, and squinting.

Between her two eyes an excrescence arose,
Which the vulgar call snout, but which I call a nose;
An emblem of sense, it should seem to appear,
For without one we'd look very foolish and queer:
 With your Roman, Grecian, snub-nose, pug-nose, snuffling snout, and
 sneezing.

Good-natured she look'd, that's when out of a frown,
And blush'd like a rose—when the paint was put on;
At church ev'ry morning her prayers she could scan,
And each night sigh and think of—the duty of man,
 With her groaning, moaning, sighing, dying, tabernacle—love-feasts.

The follies of youth she had long given o'er,
For the virgin I sing of—was turn'd fifty-four:
Yet suitors she had, who, with words sweet as honey,
Strove hard to possess the bright charms of her money,
 With her household, leasehold, freehold, and her copyhold and tenement.

The first who appear'd on this am'rous list,
Was a tailor, who swore by his thimble and twist,
That if his strong passion she e'er should refuse,
He'd depart from the world, shop, cabbage, and goose,
 With his waistcoat, breeches, measures, scissors, button-holes and buckram.

The next was a butcher, of slaughter-ox fame,
A very great boor, and Dick Hog was his name;
He swore she was lamb—but she laugh'd at his pains,
For she hated calf's head—unless served up with brains.
 With his sheep's head, lamb's fry, chitterlins—his marrow-bones and cleavers.

After many debates, which occasion'd much strife,
'Mongst love-sick admirers to make her their wife,
To end each dispute came a man out of breath,
Who eloped with the maid, and his name was grim Death.
 With his pick-axe, sexton, coffin, funeral, skeleton, and bone-house.

Anonymous

THE WHANGO TREE

The woggly bird sat on the whango tree,
    Nooping the rinkum corn,
And graper and graper, alas! grew he,
    And cursed the day he was born.
His crute was clum and his voice was rum,
    As curiously thus sang he,
"Oh, would I'd been rammed and eternally clammed
    Ere I perched on this whango tree."

Now the whango tree had a bubbly thorn,
    As sharp as a nootie's bill,
And it stuck in the woggly bird's umptum lorn
    And weepadge, the smart did thrill.
He fumbled and cursed, but that wasn't the worst,
    For he couldn't at all get free,
And he cried, "I am gammed, and injustibly nammed
    On the luggardly whango tree."

And there he sits still, with no worm in his bill,
    Nor no guggledom in his nest;
He is hungry and bare, and gobliddered with care,
    And his grabbles give him no rest;
He is weary and sore and his tugmut is soar,
    And nothing to nob has he,
As he chirps, "I am blammed and corruptibly jammed,
    In this cuggerdom whango tree."

Anonymous (1840)

LIMERICK

Cleopatra, who thought they maligned her,
Resolved to reform and be kinder;
    "If, when pettish," she said,
    "I should knock off your head,
Won't you give me some gentle reminder?"

Newton Mackintosh

MISFORTUNES
NEVER COME SINGLY

Making toast at the fireside,
Nurse fell in the grate and died;
And, what makes it ten times worse,
All the toast was burned with Nurse.

Col. D. Streamer

THE WALLOPING WINDOW-BLIND

A capital ship for an ocean trip
    Was the "Walloping Window-blind"—
No gale that blew dismayed her crew
    Or troubled the captain's mind.
The man at the wheel was taught to feel
    Contempt for the wildest blow,
And it often appeared, when the weather had cleared,
    That he'd been in his bunk below.

The boatswain's mate was very sedate,
    Yet fond of amusement, too;
And he played hop-scotch with the starboard watch,
    While the captain tickled the crew.
And the gunner we had was apparently mad,
    For he sat on the after rail,
And fired salutes with the captain's boots,
    In the teeth of the booming gale.

The captain sat in a commodore's hat
    And dined in a royal way
On toasted pigs and pickles and figs
    And gummery bread each day.
But the cook was Dutch and behaved as such:
    For the food that he gave the crew
Was a number of tons of hot-cross buns
    Chopped up with sugar and glue.

And we all felt ill as mariners will,
    On a diet that's cheap and rude;
And we shivered and shook as we dipped the cook
    In a tub of his gluesome food.
Then nautical pride we laid aside,
    And we cast the vessel ashore
On the Gulliby Isles, where the Poohpooh smiles,
    And the Anagazanders roar.

Composed of sand was that favored land,
    And trimmed with cinnamon straws;
And pink and blue was the pleasing hue
    Of the Tickletoeteaser's claws.
And we sat on the edge of a sandy ledge
    And shot at the whistling bee;
And the Binnacle-bats wore water-proof hats
    As they danced in the sounding sea.

On rubagub bark, from dawn to dark,
    We fed, till we all had grown
Uncommonly shrunk,—when a Chinese junk
    Came by from the torriby zone.
She was stubby and square, but we didn't much care,
    And we cheerily put to sea;
And we left the crew of the junk to chew
    The bark of the rubagub tree.

Charles Edward Carryl (1842–1920)

LIMERICK

There once was an old man of Lyme
Who married three wives at a time;
    When asked, "Why a third?"
    He replied, "One's absurd!
And bigamy, sir, is a crime."

William Cosmo Monkhouse (1840–1901)

THE BROWNIES
SOWING THE SEED

The cunning Brownies met one night
To talk about an upward flight.
Said one: "The old balloon no more
Attracts the crowds as heretofore;
Without a helm or guiding wheel,
In those one must misgivings feel,
When up above the clouds they pass,
Clean out of sight of woods and grass.
But where one has control of speed,
And power to turn in time of need,
Go where you like, rise when you please,
And settle down again with ease.

·   ·   ·   ·   ·

Said he: " 'T is not enough to sail
Across the sky, o'er hill and vale,
For pleasure's sake, but we must do
Some good as we our way pursue.
The country's ready for the grain;
The fields are plowed, and moist with rain;
Now drop a seed upon the ground,
And it will sprout ere day goes round.
We'll choose all kinds of seed with care
To scatter well through upper air,
While drifting over vale and hill,
And let it settle where it will."

·   ·   ·   ·   ·

Palmer Cox (1840–1924)

96

BALLAD OF BEDLAM

Oh, lady, wake! the azure moon
  Is rippling in the verdant skies,
The owl is warbling his soft tune,
  Awaiting but thy snowy eyes.
The joys of future years are past,
  To-morrow's hopes have fled away;
Still let us love, and e'en at last
  We shall be happy yesterday.

The early beam of rosy night
  Drives off the ebon morn afar,
While through the murmur of the light
  The huntsman winds his mad guitar.
Then, lady, wake! my brigantine
  Pants, neighs, and prances to be free;
Till the creation I am thine,
  To some rich desert fly with me.

From Punch

THE CRUISE OF THE "P. C."

Across the swiffling waves they went,
  The gumly bark yoked to and fro;
The jupple crew on pleasure bent,
  Galored, "This is a go!"

Beside the poo's'l stood the Gom,
  He chirked and murgled in his glee;
While near him, in a grue jipon,
  The Bard was quite at sea.

"Gallop! Golloy! Thou scrumjous Bard!
  Take pen (thy stylo) and endite
A pome, my brain needs kurgling hard,
  And I will feast tonight."

That wansome Bard he took his pen,
  A flirgly look around he guv;
He squoffled once, he squirled, and then
  He wrote what's writ above.

Anonymous

COSSIMBAZAR

Come fleetly, come fleetly, my hookabadar,
For the sound of the tam-tam is heard from afar.
"Banoolah! Banoolah!" The Brahmins are nigh,
And the depths of the jungle re-echo their cry.
   Pestonjee Bomanjee!
   Smite the guitar;
Join in the chorus, my hookabadar.

Heed not the blast of the deadly monsoon,
Nor the blue Brahmaputra that gleams in the moon.
Stick to thy music, and oh, let the sound
Be heard with distinctness a mile or two round.
   Jamsetjee, Jeejeebhoy!
   Sweep the guitar.
Join in the chorus, my hookabadar.

   • • • • •

Henry S. Leigh (1837–1883)

KINDNESS TO ANIMALS

Speak gently to the herring and kindly to the calf,
Be blithesome with the bunny, at barnacles don't laugh!
Give nuts unto the monkey, and buns unto the bear,
Ne'er hint at currant jelly if you chance to see a hare!
Oh, little girls, pray hide your combs when tortoises draw nigh,
And never in the hearing of a pigeon whisper Pie!
But give the stranded jelly-fish a shove into the sea, —
Be always kind to animals wherever you may be!

Oh, make not game of sparrows, nor faces at the ram,
And ne'er allude to mint sauce when calling on a lamb.
Don't beard the thoughtful oyster, don't dare the cod to crimp.
Don't cheat the pike, or ever try to pot the playful shrimp.
Tread lightly on the turning worm, don't bruise the butterfly,
Don't ridicule the wry-neck, nor sneer at salmon-fry;
Oh, ne'er delight to make dogs fight, nor bantams disagree, —
Be always kind to animals wherever you may be!

Be lenient with lobsters, and ever kind to crabs,
And be not disrespectful to cuttle-fish or dabs;
Chase not the Cochin-China, chaff not the ox obese,
And babble not of feather-beds in company with geese.
Be tender with the tadpole, and let the limpet thrive,
Be merciful to mussels, don't skin your eels alive;
When talking to a turtle don't mention calipee—
Be always kind to animals wherever you may be.

Joseph Ashby-Sterry (18??–1917)

THE LUGUBRIOUS WHING-WHANG

Out on the margin of moonshine land,
  Tickle me, love, in these lonesome ribs,
Out where the whing-whang loves to stand,
Writing his name with his tail on the sand,
And wiping it out with his oogerish hand;
  Tickle me, love, in these lonesome ribs.

Is it the gibber of gungs and keeks?
  Tickle me, love, in these lonesome ribs,
Or what *is* the sound the whing-whang seeks,
Crouching low by the winding creeks,
And holding his breath for weeks and weeks?
  Tickle me, love, in these lonesome ribs.

Anoint him the wraithest of wraithly things!
  Tickle me, love, in these lonesome ribs,
'T is a fair whing-whangess with phosphor rings,
And bridal jewels of fangs and stings,
And she sits and as sadly and softly sings
As the mildewed whir of her own dead wings;
  Tickle me, dear; tickle me here;
  Tickle me, love, in these lonesome ribs.

James Whitcomb Riley (1849–1916)

NEPHELIDIA

From the depth of the dreamy decline of the dawn through a notable nimbus of
  nebulous noonshine,
Pallid and pink as the palm of the flag-flower that flickers with fear of the flies as
  they float,
Are they looks of our lovers that lustrously lean from a marvel of mystic miracu-
  lous moonshine,
These that we feel in the blood of our blushes that thicken and threaten with
  sobs from the throat?
Thicken and thrill as a theatre thronged at appeal of an actor's appalled agitation,
Fainter with fear of the fires of the future than pale with the promise of pride
  in the past;
Flushed with the famishing fulness of fever that reddens with radiance of rathe
  recreation,

Gaunt as the ghastliest of glimpses that gleam through the gloom of the gloaming
  when ghosts go aghast?
Nay, for the nick of the tick of the time is a tremulous touch on the temples of
  terror,
Strained as the sinews yet strenuous with strife of the dead who is dumb as the
  dust-heaps of death:
Surely no soul is it, sweet as the spasm of erotic emotional exquisite error,
Bathed in the balms of beatified bliss, beatific itself by beatitude's breath.
Surely no spirit or sense of a soul that was soft to the spirit and soul of our senses
Sweetens the stress of suspiring suspicion that sobs in the semblance and sound
  of a sigh;
Only this oracle opens Olympian, in mystical moods and triangular tenses—
Life is the lust of a lamp for the light that is dark till the dawn of the day when
  we die.
Mild is the mirk and monotonous music of memory melodiously mute as it
  may be,
While the hope in the heart of a hero is bruised by the breach of men's rapiers
  resigned to the rod;
Made meek as a mother whose bosom-beats bound with the bliss-bringing bulk
  of a balm-breathing baby,
As they grope through the grave-yards of creeds, under skies growing green at a
  groan for the grimness of God.
Blank is the book of his bounty beholden of old and its binding is blacker than
  bluer:
Out of blue into black is the scheme of the skies, and their dews are the wine of
  the bloodshed of things;
Till the darkling desire of delight shall be free as a fawn that is freed from the
  fangs that pursue her,
Till the heart-beats of hell shall be hushed by a hymn from the hunt that has
  harried the kernel of kings.

Algernon Swinburne (1837–1909)

POOR BROTHER

How very sad it is to think
  Our poor benighted brother
Should have his head upon one end,
  His feet upon the other.

Anonymous

MR. AND MRS. VITE'S JOURNEY

A vorthy cit, von Vitsunday,
Vith vife, rode out in vone-horse chay;
And down the streets as they did trot,
Says Mrs. Vite, "I'll tell you vat,
    Dear Villiam Vite,
    'Tis my delight,
Ven our veek's bills ve stick 'em,
    That side by side
    Ve thus should ride
To Vindsor or Vest Vickham."

"My loving vife, full vell you know,
Ve used to ride to Valthamstow,
And now I think it much the best
That ve should ride tovards the vest.
    If you agree,
    Dear vife, vith me,
And vish to change the scene;
    And, ven the dust
    Excites our thirst,
Ve'll stop at Valham Green."

"Oh, then," says Mrs. Vite, says she,
"Vat pleases you, must sure please me;
But veekly vorkins all must go,
If ve this day go cheerful through:
    For vel I loves
    The voods and groves,
They raptures put me in;
    For you know, Vite,
    Von Vitsun night,
You did my poor heart vin."

Then Mrs. Vite she took the vip,
And vack'd poor Dobbin on the hip;
Vich made him from a valk run fast,
And reach the long-vish't sign at last.
    Lo, ven they stopt,
    Out vaiter popt,
"Vat vou'd you vish to take?"

Said Vite, vith grin,
"I'll take some gin,
My vife takes vine and cake."

Mrs. Vite she having took her vine,
To Vindsor on they vent to dine:
Ven dinner o'er, Mr. Vite did talk,
"My darling vife, ve'll take a valk:
    The path is vide,
    Bq vater's side,
So ve vill valk together;
    Vile they gets tea
    For you and me,
Ve vill enjoy the veather."

Some vanton Eton boys there vere,
Vho mark'd for vaggery this pair:
Mrs. Vite cries out, "Vat are they ater?"
Ven in they popt Vite in the vater.
    The vicked vits
    Then left the cits,
Ven Vite the vaves sunk under;
    She vept, she squall'd,
    She vail'd, she bawl'd,
"Vill not none help, I vonder."

Her vimpering vords assistance brought,
Then, with a boat-hook, Vite they sought;
Ven she, vith expectation big,
Thought Vite was found, but 'twas his vig.
    Vite was not found,
    For he vas drown'd:
To stop her grief each bid her;
    "Ah! no," she cry'd,
    "I vas a bride,
But now I is a vidor."

Anonymous

THE CRANKADOX

The Crankadox leaned o'er the edge of the moon,
    And wistfully gazed on the sea
Where the Gryxabodill madly whistled a tune
    To the air of "Ti-fol-de-ding-dee."

The quavering shriek of the Fly-up-the-creek
    Was fitfully wafted afar
To the Queen of the Wunks as she powdered her cheek
    With the pulverized rays of a star.

The Gool closed his ear on the voice of the Grig,
    And his heart it grew heavy as lead
As he marked the Baldekin adjusting his wig
    On the opposite side of his head,
And the air it grew chill as the Gryxabodill
    Raised his dank, dripping fins to the skies
To plead with the Plunk for the use of her bill
    To pick the tears out of his eyes.

The ghost of the Zhack flitted by in a trance,
    And the Squidjum hid under a tub
As he heard the loud hooves of the Hooken advance
    With a rub-a-dub-dub-a-dub dub!
And the Crankadox cried as he laid down and died,
    "My fate there is none to bewail!"
While the Queen of the Wunks drifted over the tide
    With a long piece of crape to her tail.

James Whitcomb Riley (1849–1916)

MOORLANDS OF THE NOT

Across the moorlands of the Not
    We chase the gruesome When;
And hunt the Itness of the What
    Through forests of the Then.
Into the Inner Consciousness
    We track the crafty Where;
We spear the Ego tough, and beard
    The Selfhood in his lair.

With lassos of the brain we catch
    The Isness of the Was;
And in the copses of the Whence
    We hear the think bees buzz.
We climb the slippery Whichbark tree
    To watch the Thusness roll;
And pause betimes in gnostic rimes
    To woo the Over Soul.

Anonymous

SIR BUNNY FUNNY
OF WARREN-HALL

Sir Bunny is a splendid shot,
 And every time he fires,
A farmer or a keeper falls,
 Sometimes a brace of squires.

He went out shooting yesterday
 With young Lord Leveret;
But the wind it blew, and the rain it pour'd
 And both got soaking wet.

THE LAZY SHEPHERD

A shepherd and his collie-dog
 One day went fast to sleep,
And they told a great fat Poodle-thing
 To mind the silly Sheep.

POOR OLD STUPID

There lived an old man in a garret,
　　So afraid of a little tom-cat,
That he pulled himself up to the ceiling,
　　And hung himself up in his hat.

And for fear of the wind and the rain,
　　He took his umbrella to bed—
I've half an idea, that silly old man
　　Was a little bit wrong in his head.

A STUFF'D BIRD

Poor old Cockeytoo: poor old Cockeytoo:
　　He's ate so much, and drunk so much,
He don't know what to do.

　　Then take him by the tail;
　　　　But mind he doesn't bite,
　　And shake him well, until he finds
　　　　Another appetite.

D'Arcy W. Thompson (1829–1902)
Illustrations by Charles H. Bennett (1829–1867)

ON THE ROAD

Said Folly to Wisdom,
    "Pray, where are we going?"
Said Wisdom to Folly,
    "There's no way of knowing."

Said Folly to Wisdom,
    "Then what shall we do?"
Said Wisdom to Folly,
    "I thought to ask you."

        Tudor Jenks (1857–1922)

WISHES OF AN ELDERLY MAN

I wish I loved the Human Race;
I wish I loved its silly face;
I wish I liked the way it walks;
I wish I liked the way it talks;
And when I'm introduced to one
I wish I thought *What Jolly Fun!*

        Walter Raleigh (1861–1922)

TRANSCENDENTALISM

It is told, in Buddhi-theosophic schools,
    There are rules,
By observing which, when mundane labor irks
    One can simulate quiescence
    By a timely evanescence
    From his Active Mortal Essence,
      (Or his Works).

The particular procedure leaves research
    In the lurch,
But, apparently, this matter-moulded form
    Is a kind of outer plaster,
    Which a well-instructed Master
    Can remove without disaster
      When he's warm.

And to such as mourn an Indian solar clime
    At its prime
'T were a thesis most immeasurably fit,
    So expansively elastic,
    And so plausibly fantastic,
    That one gets enthusiastic
      For a bit.

        From the Times of India

COLLUSION BETWEEN A ALE-GAITER
AND A WATER-SNAIK

There is a niland on a river lying,
Which runs into Gautimaly, a warm country,
Lying near the Tropicks, covered with sand;
Hear and their a symptum of a Wilow,
Hanging of its umberagious limbs & branches
Over the clear streme meandering far below.
This was the home of the now silent Alegaiter,
When not in his other element confine'd:
Here he wood set up his eggs asleep
With 1 ey observant of flis and other passing
Objects: a while it kept a going on so:
Fereles of danger was the happy Alegaiter!
But a las! in a nevil our he was fourced to
Wake! that dreme of Blis was two sweet for him.
1 morning the sun arose with unusool splender
Whitch allso did our Alegiater, coming from the water,
His scails a flinging of the rais of the son back,
To the fountain-head which tha originly sprung from,
But having not had nothing to eat for some time, he
Was slepy and gap'd, in a short time, widely.
Unfoalding soon a welth of perl-white teth,
The rais of the son soon shet his sinister ey
Because of their mutool splendor and warmth.
The evil Our (which I sed) was now come;
Evidently a good chans for a water-snaik
Of the large specie, which soon appeared
Into the horison, near the bank where reposed
Calmly in slepe the Alegaiter before spoken of.
About 60 feet was his Length (not the 'gaiter)
And he was aperiently a well-proportioned snaik.
When he was all ashore he glared upon
The iland with approval, but was soon
"Astonished with the view and lost to wonder" (from Wats)
(For jest then he began to see the Alegaiter)
Being a nateral enemy of his'n, he worked hisself
Into a fury, also a ni position.
Before the Alegaiter well could ope
His eye (in other words perceive his danger)
The Snaik had enveloped his body just 19
Times with "foalds voluminous and vast" (from Milton)
And had tore off several scails in the confusion,
Besides squeazing him awfully into his stomoc.

Just then, by a fortinate turn in his affairs,
He ceazed into his mouth the careless tale
Of the unreflecting water-snaik! Grown desperate
He, finding that his tale was fast squesed
Terrible while they roaled all over the iland.
It was a well-conduckted Affair; no noise
Disturbed the harmony of the seen, ecsept
Onct when a Willow was snaped into by the roaling.
Eeach of the combatence hadn't a minit for holering.
So the conflick was naterally tremenjous!
But soon by grate force the tail was bit complete-
Ly of; but the eggzeration was too much
For his delicate Constitootion; he felt a compression
Onto his chest and generally over his body;
When he ecspressed his breathing, it was with
Grate difficulty that he felt inspired again onct more.
Of course this state must suffer a revolootion.
So the alegaiter give but yel, and egspired.
The water-snaik realed hisself off, & survay'd
For say 10 minits, the condition of
His fo: then wondering what made his tail hurt,
He slowly went off for to cool.

J. W. Morris

THE BUTTERFLY
THAT STAMPED

There was never a Queen like Balkis,
    From here to the wide world's end;
But Balkis talked to a butterfly
    As you would talk to a friend.

There was never a King like Solomon,
    Not since the world began;
But Solomon talked to a butterfly
    As a man would talk to a man.

She was Queen of Sabæa—
    And *he* was Asia's Lord—
But they both of 'em talked to butterflies
    When they took their walks abroad!

Rudyard Kipling (1865–1936)

NOT I

Some like drink
　　In a pint pot,
Some like to think,
　　Some not.

Strong Dutch cheese,
　　Old Kentucky Rye,
Some like these;
　　Not I.

Some like Poe,
　　And others like Scott;
Some like Mrs. Stowe,
　　Some not.

Some like to laugh,
　　Some like to cry,
Some like to chaff;
　　Not I.

Robert Louis Stevenson
(1850–1894)

MARY JANE

Mary Jane was a farmer's daughter,
　　Mary Jane did what she oughter.
She fell in love—but all in vain;
　　Oh, poor Mary! oh, poor Jane!

Anonymous

THE SONG OF MILKANWATHA

• • • • •

He killed the noble Mudjokivis.
Of the skin he made him mittens,
Made them with the fur side inside,
Made them with the skin side outside.
He, to get the warm side inside,
Put the inside skin side outside;
He, to get the cold side outside,
Put the warm side fur side inside.
That's why he put the fur side inside,
Why he put the skin side outside,
Why he turned them inside outside.

• • • • •

George A. Strong

COURTSHIP

A lobster wooed a lady crab,
    And kissed her lovely face.
"Upon my sole," the crabbess cried,
    "I wish you'd mind your plaice!"

Anonymous

LIMERICK

There was a young man at St. Kitts
Who was very much troubled with fits;
    The eclipse of the moon
    Threw him into a swoon,
When he tumbled and broke into bits.

Anonymous

THE WASH THAT STAYED
OUT ALL NIGHT

The Full Moon now and then
    Looks down on a strange sight,
But none more strange than when
    Our Wash stayed out all night.

All night it swayed and rocked
    And kicked and capered wildly;
To say the Moon was shocked
    Is to express it mildly.

The Barn Owl cried "Begosh!
    I never thought to see
A plain, God-fearing Wash
    Behave like Lingerie!"

The Rabbits, when they heard
    The rumpus, all came flocking
To join the dance. My word!
    A Bunny takes some shocking!

Oliver Herford (1863–1935)

THE DINKEY-BIRD

In an ocean, 'way out yonder
 (As all sapient people know),
Is the land of Wonder-Wander,
 Whither children love to go;
It's their playing, romping, swinging,
 That give great joy to me
While the Dinkey-Bird goes singing
 In the Amfalula-tree!

There the gum-drops grow like cherries,
 And taffy's thick as peas, —
Caramels you pick like berries
 When, and where, and how you please:
Big red sugar-plums are clinging
 To the cliffs beside that sea
Where the Dinkey-Bird is singing
 In the Amfalula-tree.

So when children shout and scamper
 And make merry all the day,
When there's naught to put a damper
 To the ardor of their play;
When I hear their laughter ringing,
 Then I'm sure as sure can be
That the Dinkey-Bird is singing
 In the Amfalula-tree.

For the Dinkey-Bird's bravuras
 And staccatos are so sweet—
His roulades, appogiaturas,
 And robustos so complete,
That the youth of every nation—
 Be they near or far away—
Have especial delectation
 In that gladsome roundelay.

Their eyes grow bright and brighter,
 Their lungs begin to crow,
Their hearts get light and lighter,
 And their cheeks are all aglow;
For an echo cometh bringing
 The news to all and me.
That the Dinkey-Bird is singing
 In the Amfalula-tree.

I'm sure you'd like to go there
 To see your feathered friend—
And so many goodies grow there
 You would like to comprehend!
Speed, little dreams, your winging
 To that land across the sea
Where the Dinkey-Bird is singing
 In the Amfalula-Tree!

Eugene Field (1850–1895)

LIMERICK

There was a young lady of Niger
Who smiled as she rode on a Tiger;
 They came back from the ride
 With the lady inside,
And the smile on the face of the Tiger.

Anonymous

LIMERICK

There was a young lady of Milton,
Who was highly disgusted with Stilton;
    When offered a bite,
    She said, "Not a mite!"
That suggestive young lady of Milton.

Anonymous

THE PESSIMIST

Nothing to do but work,
    Nothing to eat but food,
Nothing to wear but clothes
    To keep one from going nude.

Nothing to breathe but air,
    Quick as a flash 't is gone;
Nowhere to fall but off,
    Nowhere to stand but on.

Nothing to comb but hair,
    Nowhere to sleep but in bed,
Nothing to weep but tears,
    Nothing to bury but dead.

Nothing to sing but songs,
    Ah, well, alas! alack!
Nowhere to go but out,
    Nowhere to come but back.

Nothing to see but sights,
    Nothing to quench but thirst,
Nothing to have but what we've got;
    Thus thro' life we are cursed.

Nothing to strike but a gait;
    Everything moves that goes.
Nothing at all but common sense
    Can ever withstand these woes.

Ben King (1857–1894)

A TRAGEDY IN RHYME

There was a man upon a time
Who could not speak except in rhyme.
He could not voice his smallest wish,
He could not order soup or fish,
He could not hail a passing car,
He could not ask for a cigar, —
And let a rhymeless sentence mar
His speech. He could not vent despair,
Anger, or rage—he could not *swear*,

He could not even have his say
On common topics of the day.
The dreadful cold—the awful heat,
The rise in coal, the fall in wheat,
He could not rise to give his seat
In crowded car to maiden sweet,
Or buy a paper in the street, —
Except in measured, rhyming feet.
"He must have been a man of means!
In this, the age of magazines!"
I hear you say. Ah, reader, wait
Till you have heard his awful fate.
You will not then expatiate
Upon his fortune.—

      Well, one night
A burglar came, and at the sight,
The rhymester took a fearful fright.
The only avenue for flight
Was up the chimney; here he climbed
Until he stuck, and then he rhymed
As follows: —
      "Goodness gracious me!
I'm stuck as tight as tight can be!
Oh, dear, I'm in an awful plight.
I cannot budge to left or right,
Or up or down this awful chimney!"
Then he *was* stuck; had he said "Jimm'ny!"
It would have saved him many a pang.
But no! he could not stoop to slang.
In vain he writhed and racked his brain
For rhymes to "chimney."

      It was plain
He *had* to rhyme—for should he cease
He must forever hold his peace.
He tried to shout, he tried to call.
The truth fell on him like a pall.
There isn't any rhyme at all
To "chimney." —
      When they searched the room
They found it silent as a tomb.
For years they advertised in vain
They never heard of him again.

Oliver Herford (1863–1935)

CANOPUS

When quacks with pills political would dope us,
    When politics absorbs the livelong day,
I like to think about the star Canopus,
    So far, so far away.

Greatest of visioned suns, they say who list 'em;
    To weigh it science always must despair.
Its shell would hold our whole dinged solar system,
    Nor ever know 'twas there.

When temporary chairmen utter speeches,
    And frenzied henchmen howl their battle hymns,
My thoughts float out across the cosmic reaches
    To where Canopus swims.

When men are calling names and making faces,
    And all the world's ajangle and ajar,
I meditate on interstellar spaces
    And smoke a mild seegar.

For after one has had about a week of
    The arguments of friends as well as foes,
A star that has no parallax to speak of
    Conduces to repose.

Bert Leston Taylor (1866–1921)

LIMERICK

There was a young maid who said, "Why
Can't I look in my ear with my eye?
    If I give my mind to it,
    I'm sure I can do it,
You never can tell till you try."

Anonymous

THE FAMOUS BALLAD OF THE JUBILEE CUP

You may lift me up in your arms, lad, and turn my face to the sun,
For a last look back at the dear old track where the Jubilee cup was won;
And draw your chair to my side, lad—no, thank ye, I feel no pain—
For I'm going out with the tide, lad; but I'll tell you the tale again.

I'm seventy-nine or nearly, and my head it has long turned gray,
But it all comes back as clearly as though it was yesterday—
The dust, and the bookies shouting around the clerk of the scales,
And the clerk of the course, and the nobs in force, and
  'Is 'Ighness the Pr*nce of W*les.

'Twas a nine-hole thresh to wind'ard (but none of us cared for that),
With a straight run home to the service tee, and a finish along the flat,
"Stiff?" ah, well you may say it! Spot barred, and at five-stone-ten!
But at two and a bisque I'd ha' run the risk; for I was a greenhorn then.

So we stripped to the B. Race signal, the old red swallowtail—
There was young Ben Bolt and the Portland Colt, and Aston Villa, and Yale;
And W. G., and Steinitz, Leander, and The Saint,
And the G*rm*n Emp*r*r's Meteor, a-looking as fresh as paint;

John Roberts (scratch), and Safety Match, The Lascar, and Lorna Doone,
Oom Paul (a bye), and Romany Rye, and me upon Wooden Spoon;
And some of us cut for partners, and some of us strung for baulk,
And some of us tossed for stations— But there, what use to talk?

Three-quarter-back on the Kingsclere crack was station enough for me,
With a fresh jackyarder blowing and the Vicarage goal a-lee!
And I leaned and patted her centre-bit and eased the quid in her cheek,
With a "Soh my lass!" and a "Woa you brute!"—for she could do all but speak.

She was geared a thought too high perhaps; she was trained a trifle fine;
But she had the grand reach forward! I never saw such a line!
Smooth-bored, clean run, from her fiddle head with its dainty ear half-cock,
Hard-bit, *pur sang,* from her overhang to the heel of her off hind sock.

Sir Robert he walked beside me as I worked her down to the mark;
"There's money on this, my lad," said he, "and most of 'em's running dark;
But ease the sheet if you're bunkered, and pack the scrummages tight,
And use your slide at the distance, and we'll drink to your health to-night!"

But I bent and tightened my stretcher. Said I to myself, said I—
"John Jones, this here is the Jubilee Cup, and you have to do or die."
And the words weren't hardly spoken when the umpire shouted "Play!"
And we all kicked off from the Gasworks End with a "Yoicks!" and a "Gone Away!"

And at first I thought of nothing, as the clay flew by in lumps,
But stuck to the old Ruy Lopez, and wondered who'd call for trumps,
And luffed her close to the cushion, and watched each one as it broke,
And in triple file up the Rowley Mile we went like a trail of smoke.

The Lascar made the running but he didn't amount to much,
For old Oom Paul was quick on the ball, and headed it back to touch;
And the whole first flight led off with the right as The Saint took up the pace,
And drove it clean to the putting green and trumped it there with an ace.

John Roberts had given a miss in baulk, but Villa cleared with a punt;
And keeping her service hard and low the Meteor forged to the front;
With Romany Rye to windward at dormy and two to play,
And Yale close up—but a Jubilee Cup isn't run for every day.

We laid our course for the Warner—I tell you the pace was hot!
And again off Tattenham Corner a blanket covered the lot.
Check side! Check side! now steer her wide! and barely an inch of room,
With The Lascar's tail over our lee rail and brushing Leander's boom.

We were running as strong as ever—eight knots—but it couldn't last;
For the spray and the bails were flying, the whole field tailing fast;
And the Portland Colt had shot his bolt, and Yale was bumped at the Doves,
And The Lascar resigned to Steinitz, stalemated in fifteen moves.

It was bellows to mend with Roberts—starred three for a penalty kick:
But he chalked his cue and gave 'em the butt, and Oom Paul marked the trick—
"Offside—No Ball—and at fourteen all! Mark Cock! and two for his nob!"
When W. G. ran clean through his lee and beat him twice with a lob.

He yorked him twice on a crumbling pitch and wiped his eye with a brace,
But his guy-rope split with the strain of it and he dropped back out of the race;
And I drew a bead on the Meteor's lead, and challenging none too soon,
Bent over and patted her garboard strake, and called upon Wooden Spoon.

She was all of a shiver forward, the spoondrift thick on her flanks,
But I'd brought her an easy gambit, and nursed her over the banks;
She answered her helm—the darling! and woke up now with a rush,
While the Meteor's jock, he sat like a rock—he knew we rode for his brush!

There was no one else left in it. The Saint was using his whip,
And Safety Match, with a lofting catch, was pocketed deep at slip;
And young Ben Bolt with his niblick took miss at Leander's lunge,
But topped the net with the ricochet, and Steinitz threw up the sponge.

But none of the lot could stop the rot—nay, don't ask *me* to stop!
The villa had called for lemons, Oom Paul had taken his drop,
And both were kicking the referee. Poor fellow! he done his best;
But, being in doubt, he'd ruled them out—which he always did when pressed.

So, inch by inch, I tightened the winch, and chucked the sandbags out—
I heard the nursery cannons pop, I heard the bookies shout:
"The Meteor wins!" "No, Wooden Spoon!" "Check!" "Vantage!" "Leg Before!"
"Last Lap!" "Pass Nap!" At his saddle-flap I put up the helm and wore.

You may overlap at the saddle-flap, and yet be loo'd on the tape:
And it all depends upon changing ends, how a seven-year-old will shape;
It was tack and tack to the Lepe and back—a fair ding-dong to the Ridge,
And he led by his forward canvas yet as we shot 'neath Hammersmith Bridge.

He led by his forward canvas—he led from his strongest suit—
But along we went on a roaring scent, and at Fawley I gained a foot.
He fisted off with his jigger, and gave me his wash—too late!
Deuce—Vantage—Check! By neck and neck we rounded into the straight.

I could hear the "Conquering 'Ero" a-crashing on Godfrey's band,
And my hopes fell sudden to zero, just there, with the race in hand—
In sight of the Turf's Blue Ribbon, in sight of the umpire's tape,
As I felt the tack of her spinnaker c-rack! as I heard the steam escape!

Had I lost at that awful juncture my presence of mind? . . . but no!
I leaned and felt for the puncture, and plugged it there with my toe . . .
Hand over hand by the Members' Stand I lifted and eased her up,
Shot—clean and fair—to the crossbar there, and landed the Jubilee Cup!

"The odd by a head, and leg before," so the Judge he gave the word:
And the umpire shouted "Over!" but I neither spoke nor stirred.
They crowded round: for there on the ground I lay in a dead-cold swoon,
Pitched neck and crop on the turf atop of my beautiful Wooden Spoon.

Her dewlap tire was punctured, her bearings all red hot;
She'd a lolling tongue, and her bowsprit sprung, and her running gear in a knot;
And amid the sobs of her backers, Sir Robert loosened her girth
And led her away to the knacker's. She had raced her last on earth!

But I mind me well of the tear that fell from the eye of our noble Pr*nce,
And the things he said as he tucked me in bed—and I've lain there ever since;
Tho' it all gets mixed up queerly that happened before my spill, —
But I draw my thousand yearly: it'll pay for the doctor's bill.

I'm going out with the tide, lad—you'll dig me a humble grave,
And whiles you will bring your bride, lad, and your sons, if sons you have,
And there when the dews are weeping, and the echoes murmur "Peace!"
And the salt, salt tide comes creeping and covers the popping-crease;

In the hour when the ducks deposit their eggs with a boasted force,
They'll look and whisper "How was it?" and you'll take them over the course,
And your voice will break as you try to speak of the glorious first of June,
When the Jubilee Cup, with John Jones up, was won upon Wooden Spoon.

Arthur T. Quiller-Couch (1863–1944)

VERSES

I'd rather have habits than clothes,
For that's where my intellect shows.
    And as for my hair,
    Do you think I should care
To comb it at night with my toes?

I wish that my Room had a Floor;
I don't so much care for a Door,
    But this walking around
    Without touching the ground
Is getting to be quite a bore!

Gelett Burgess (1866–1951)

THE PURPLE COW

I never saw a Purple Cow,
 I never hope to see one;
But I can tell you, anyhow,
 I'd rather see than be one.

Gelett Burgess (1866–1951)

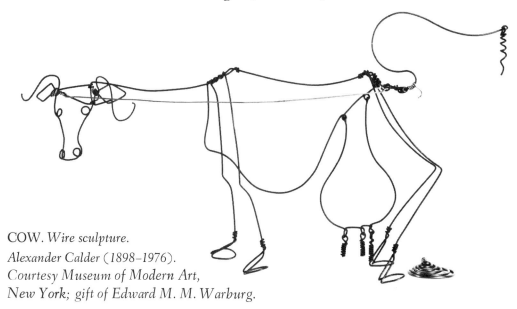

COW. *Wire sculpture.*
Alexander Calder (1898–1976).
Courtesy Museum of Modern Art,
New York; gift of Edward M. M. Warburg.

THE DOG IN THE MANGER

A churlish, pampered Cur, who had a comfortable place in a gentleman's well-filled Manger, would from thence snap and snarl to frighten off all poor beasts of draught and burden who passed that way—driven by the hardness of the time of year to beg for provender they could not earn by labour in the fields. This Dog wanted for nothing himself, and yet took an ill-natured pleasure in keeping poor famishing creatures from many a meal, which, but for his officious yelping, they might have enjoyed from his Master's bounty.

MORAL

There would be sunshine in many a poor man's house, but for officious, go-between window-shutters.

Charles H. Bennett (1829–1867)

There was an Old Man who said "Hush!
When they said, "Is it small?"
It is four times

There was an Old Man with an Owl, who continued to bother and howl;
He sat on a rail and imbibed bitter ale,
Which refreshed that Old Man and his Owl.

Edward Lear (1812–1888)

perceive a young bird in this bush!"
He replied, "Not at all!
s big as the bush!"

There was an Old Person whose habits induced him to feed upon Rabbits;
When he'd eaten eighteen, he turned perfectly green,
Upon which he relinquished those habits.

THE GOSSIPS. *Arthur Rackham* (1867–1939)

THE CURSE

*To a sister of an enemy of the author's,
  who disapproved of* The Playboy

Lord, confound this surly sister,
Blight her brow with blotch and blister,
Cramp her larynx, lung, and liver,
In her guts a galling give her.

Let her live to earn her dinners
In Mountjoy with seedy sinners:
Lord, this judgement quickly bring,
And I'm your servant, J. M. Synge.

J. M. Synge (1871–1909)

LITTLE WILLIE

Little Willie hung his sister,
    She was dead before we missed her.
"Willie's always up to tricks!
    Ain't he cute? He's only six!"

Anonymous

THE FAIRY FIDDLER

'Tis I go fiddling, fiddling,
    By weedy ways forlorn:
I make the blackbird's music
    Ere in his breast 'tis born:
The sleeping larks I waken
    'Twixt the midnight and the morn.

No man alive has seen me,
    But women hear me play
Sometimes at the door or window,
    Fiddling the souls away, —
The child's soul and the colleen's
    Out of the covering clay.

None of my fairy kinsmen
    Make music with me now;
Alone the raths I wander
    Or ride the whitethorn bough;
But the wild swans they know me,
    And the horse that draws the plough.

Nora Hopper (1871–1906)

HERE IS THE TALE

After Rudyard Kipling

Here is the tale—and you must make the most of it!
Here is the rhyme—ah, listen and attend!
Backwards—forwards—read it all and boast of it
If you are anything the wiser at the end!

Now Jack looked up—it was time to sup, and the bucket was yet to fill,
And Jack looked round for a space and frowned, then beckoned his sister Jill,
And twice he pulled his sister's hair, and thrice he smote her side;
"Ha' done, ha' done with your impudent fun—ha' done with your games!" she
    cried;
"You have made mud-pies of a marvellous size—finger and face are black,
You have trodden the Way of the Mire and Clay—now up and wash you, Jack!
Or else, or ever we reach our home, there waiteth an angry dame—
Well you know the weight of her blow—the supperless open shame!
Wash, if you will, on yonder hill—wash, if you will, at the spring, —
Or keep your dirt, to your certain hurt, and an imminent walloping!"

"You must wash—you must scrub—you must scrape!" growled Jack, "you must
    traffic with cans and pails,
Nor keep the spoil of the good brown soil in the rim of your finger-nails!
The morning path you must tread to your bath—you must wash ere the night
    descends,
And all for the cause of conventional laws and the soapmakers' dividends!
But if 't is sooth that our meal in truth depends on our washing, Jill,
By the sacred right of our appetite—haste—haste to the top of the hill!"

They have trodden the Way of the Mire and Clay, they have toiled and trav-
    elled far,
They have climbed to the brow of the hill-top now, where the bubbling foun-
    tains are,
They have taken the bucket and filled it up—yea, filled it up to the brim;
But Jack he sneered at his sister Jill, and Jill she jeered at him:
"What, blown already!" Jack cried out (and his was a biting mirth!)
"You boast indeed of your wonderful speed—but what is the boasting worth?
Now, if you can run as the antelope runs, and if you can turn like a hare,
Come, race me, Jill, to the foot of the hill—and prove your boasting fair!"

"Race? What is a race" (and a mocking face had Jill as she spake the word)
"Unless for a prize the runner tries? The truth indeed ye heard,
For I can run as the antelope runs, and I can turn like a hare: —
The first one down wins half-a-crown—and I will race you there!"

"Yea, if for the lesson that you will learn (the lesson of humbled pride)
The price you fix at two-and-six, it shall not be denied;
Come, take your stand at my right hand, for here is the mark we toe:
Now, are you ready, and are you steady? Gird up your petticoats! Go!"

And Jill she ran like a winging bolt, a bolt from the bow released,
But Jack like a stream of the lightning gleam, with its pathway duly greased;
He ran down hill in front of Jill like a summer-lightning flash—
Till he suddenly tripped on a stone, or slipped, and fell to the earth with a crash.
Then straight did rise on his wondering eyes the constellations fair,
Arcturus and the Pleiades, the Greater and Lesser Bear,
The swirling rain of a comet's train he saw, as he swiftly fell—
And Jill came tumbling after him with a loud triumphant yell:
"You have won, you have won, the race is done! And as for the wager laid—
You have fallen down with a broken crown—the half-crown debt is paid!"

They have taken Jack to the room at the back where the family medicines are,
And he lies in bed with a broken head in a halo of vinegar;
While, in that Jill had laughed her fill as her brother fell to earth,
She had felt the sting of a walloping—she hath paid the price of her mirth!

Here is the tale—and now you have the whole of it,
Here is the story—well and wisely planned,
Beauty—Duty—these make up the soul of it—
But, ah, my little readers, will you mark and understand?

Anthony C. Deane (1870–1946)

SUSAN

Susan poisoned her grandmother's tea;
  Grandmamma died in agonee.
Susan's papa was greatly vexed,
  And he said to Susan, "My dear, what next?"

Anonymous

JIM,

Who ran away from his Nurse,
and was eaten by a Lion.

There was a Boy whose name was Jim;
His Friends were very good to him.
They gave him Tea, and Cakes, and Jam
And slices of delicious Ham,
And Chocolate with pink inside,
And little Tricycles to ride,
And read him Stories through and through,
And even took him to the Zoo—
But there it was the dreadful Fate
Befell him, which I now relate.

You know—at least you ought to know,
For I have often told you so—
That Children never are allowed
To leave their Nurses in a Crowd;
Now this was Jim's especial Foible,
He ran away when he was able,
And on this inauspicious day
He slipped his hand and ran away!
He hadn't gone a yard when—Bang!
With open Jaws, a Lion sprang,
And hungrily began to eat
The Boy: beginning at his feet.

The Lion made a sudden Stop,
He let the Dainty Morsel drop,
And slunk reluctant to his Cage,
Snarling with Disappointed Rage.
But when he bent him over Him
The Honest Keeper's Eyes were dim.
The Lion having reached his Head,
The Miserable Boy was dead!

Now just imagine how it feels
When first your toes and then your heels,
And then by gradual degrees,
Your shins and ankles, calves and knees,
Are slowly eaten, bit by bit.
No wonder Jim detested it!
No wonder that he shouted "Hi!"
The Honest Keeper heard his cry,
Though very fat he almost ran
To help the little gentleman.
"Ponto!" he ordered as he came
(For Ponto was the Lion's name),
"Ponto!" he cried, with angry Frown.
"Let go, Sir! Down, Sir! Put it down!"

When Nurse informed his Parents, they
Were more Concerned than I can say:—
His Mother, as She dried her eyes,
Said, "Well—it gives me no surprise,
He would not do as he was told!"
His Father, who was self-controlled,
Bade all the children round attend
To James' miserable end,
And always keep a-hold of Nurse
For fear of finding something worse.

Hilaire Belloc (1870–1953)
Drawings by B. T. B.
(Lord Ian B. G. T. Blackwood, 1870–1917)

REBECCA,

*Who slammed Doors for Fun
and Perished Miserably.*

A Trick that everyone abhors
In Little Girls is slamming Doors,
A Wealthy Banker's Little Daughter
Who lived in Palace Green, Bayswater
(By name Rebecca Offendort),
Was given to this Furious Sport.

She would deliberately go
And Slam the door like Billy-Ho!
To make her Uncle Jacob start.
She was not really bad at heart,
But only rather rude and wild:
She was an aggravating child . . .

It happened that a Marble Bust
Of Abraham was standing just
Above the Door this little Lamb
Had carefully prepared to Slam,
And Down it came! It knocked her flat!
It laid her out! She looked like that.

Her funeral Sermon (which was long
And followed by a Sacred Song)
Mentioned her Virtues, it is true,
But dwelt upon her Vices too,
And showed the Dreadful End of One
Who goes and slams the door for Fun.

The children who were brought to hear
The awful Tale from far and near
Were much impressed, and inly swore
They never more would slam the Door.
—As often they had done before.

Hilaire Belloc (1870–1953)
Drawings by B. T. B.
(Lord Ian B. G. T. Blackwood, 1870–1917)

133

ALGERNON,

Who played with a Loaded Gun,
and, on missing his Sister
was reprimanded by his Father.

Young Algernon, the Doctor's Son,
Was playing with a Loaded Gun
He pointed it towards his sister,
Aimed very carefully, but Missed her!
His Father, who was standing near,
The Loud Explosion chanced to Hear,
And reprimanded Algernon
For playing with a Loaded Gun.

Hilaire Belloc (1870–1953)
Drawings by B. T. B.
(Lord Ian B. G. T. Blackwood, 1870–1917)

LINES TO MISS FLORENCE
HUNTINGDON

Sweet maiden of Passamaquoddy,
    Shall we seek for communion of souls
Where the deep Mississippi meanders,
    Or the distant Saskatchewan rolls?

Ah no, —for in Maine I will find thee
    A sweetly sequestrated nook,
Where the far-winding Skoodoowabskooksis
    Conjoins with the Skoodoowabskook.

There wander two beautiful rivers,
    With many a winding and crook;
The one is the Skoodoowabskooksis,
    The other—the Skoodoowabskook.

Ah, sweetest of haunts! though unmentioned
    In geography, atlas, or book,
How fair is the Skoodoowabskooksis,
    When joining the Skoodoowabskook!

Our cot shall be close by the waters
    Within that sequestrated nook—
Reflected in Skoodoowabskooksis
    And mirrored in Skoodoowabskook.

You shall sleep to the music of leaflets,
    By zephyrs in wantonness shook,
And dream of the Skoodoowabskooksis,
    And, perhaps, of the Skoodoowabskook.

When awaked by the hens and the roosters,
    Each morn, you shall joyously look
On the junction of Skoodoowabskooksis
    With the soft gliding Skoodoowabskook.

Your food shall be fish from the waters,
    Drawn forth on the point of a hook,
From murmuring Skoodoowabskooksis,
    Or wandering Skoodoowabskook!

You shall quaff the most sparkling of water,
    Drawn forth from a silvery brook
Which flows to the Skoodoowabskooksis,
    And then to the Skoodoowabskook!

And you shall preside at the banquet,
    And I will wait on thee as cook;
And we'll talk of the Skoodoowabskooksis,
    And sing of the Skoodoowabskook!

Let others sing loudly of Saco,
    Of Quoddy, and Tattamagouche,
Of Kennebeccasis, and Quaco,
    Of Merigonishe, and Buctouche,

Of Nashwaak, and Magaguadavique,
    Or Memmerimammericook, —
There's none like the Skoodoowabskooksis,
    Excepting the Skoodoowabskook!

Anonymous

THE SINGULAR SANGFROID
OF BABY BUNTING

Bartholomew Benjamin Bunting
    Had only three passions in life,
And one of the trio was hunting,
    The others his babe and his wife.
And always, so rigid his habits,
    He frolicked at home until two,
And then started hunting for rabbits,
    And hunted till fall of the dew.

Belinda Bellonia Bunting,
    Thus widowed for half of the day,
Her duty maternal confronting,
    With baby would patiently play.
When thus was her energy wasted,
    A patented food she'd dispense.
(She had bought it the day that they pasted
    The posters all over her fence.)

But Bonaparte Buckingham Bunting,
    The infant thus blindly adored,
Replied to her worship by grunting,
    Which showed he was brutally bored.
'Twas little he cared for the troubles
    Of life. Like a crab on the sands,
From his sweet little mouth he blew bubbles,
    And threatened the air with his hands.

Bartholomew Benjamin Bunting
    One night, as his wife let him in,
Produced as the fruit of his hunting
    A cottontail's velvety skin,
Which, seeing young Bonaparte wriggle,
    He gave him without a demur,
And the babe with an aqueous giggle
    He swallowed the whole of the fur!

Belinda Bellonia Bunting
    Behaved like a consummate loon:
Her offspring in frenzy confronting
    She screamed herself mottled maroon:
She felt of his vertebræ spinal,
    Expecting he'd surely succumb,
And gave him one vigorous, final,
    Hard prod in the pit of his tum.

But Bonaparte Buckingham Bunting,
    At first but a trifle perplexed,
By a change in his manner of grunting
    Soon showed he was horribly vexed.
He displayed not a sign of repentance
    But spoke, in a dignified tone,
The only consecutive sentence
    He uttered. 'Twas: "Lemme alone."

The Moral: The parent that uses
    Precaution his folly regrets:
An infant gets all that he chooses,
    An infant chews all that he gets.
And colics? He constantly has 'em
    So long as his food is the best,
But he'll swallow with never a spasm
    What ostriches couldn't digest.

Guy Wetmore Carryl (1873–1904)

ON A FLIMMERING FLOOM YOU SHALL RIDE

Summary and footnote of and on the testimony of the poet MacLeish under appointment as Assistant Secretary of State, under oath before a congressional examining committee pressing him to divulge the portents and meanings of his poems.

Nobody noogers the shaff of a sloo.
Nobody slimbers a wench with a winch
Nor higgles armed each with a niggle
    and each the flimdrat of a smee,
    each the inbiddy hum of a smoo.

Then slong me dorst with the flagdarsh.
Then creep me deep with the crawbright.
Let idle winds ploodaddle the dorshes.
And you in the gold of the gloaming
You shall be sloam with the hoolriffs.

On a flimmering floom you shall ride.
They shall tell you bedish and desist.
On a flimmering floom you shall ride.

Carl Sandburg (1878–1967)

CLERIHEW

"I quite realized," said Columbus,
"That the earth was not a rhombus,
But I *am* a little annoyed
To find it an oblate spheroid."

Edmund Clerihew Bentley
(1875–1976)

LIMERICK

There was a young lady named Bright
Whose speed was far faster than light;
    In a relative way,
      She set out one day
And returned home the previous night.

Arthur Buller (1874–1944)

137

THE NEW HUMANE COW-CATCHER.

INGENIOUS CONTRIVANCE FOR PICKING UP THE
DRIVER'S BREAKFAST WITHOUT STOPPING THE TRAIN.

THE FIRST BATHING COMPARTMENT.

A BUSMAN'S HOLIDAY.

William Heath Robinson (1872–1944)

THE CUMBERBUNCE

I strolled beside the shining sea,
I was as lonely as could be;
No one to cheer me in my walk
But stones and sand, which cannot talk—
Sand and stones and bits of shell,
Which never have a thing to tell.

But as I sauntered by the tide
I saw a something at my side,
A something green, and blue, and pink,
And brown, and purple, too, I think.
I would not say how large it was;
I would not venture that, because
It took me rather by surprise,
And I have not the best of eyes.

Should you compare it to a cat,
I'd say it was as large as that;
Or should you ask me if the thing
Was smaller than a sparrow's wing,
I should be apt to think you knew,
And simply answer, "Very true!"

Well, as I looked upon the thing,
It murmured, "Please, sir, can I sing?"
And then I knew its name at once—
It plainly was a Cumberbunce.

You are amazed that I could tell
The creature's name so quickly? Well,
I knew it was not a paper-doll,
A pencil or a parasol,
A tennis-racket or a cheese,
And, as it was not one of these,
And I am not a perfect dunce—
It had to be a Cumberbunce!

With pleading voice and tearful eye
It seemed as though about to cry.
It looked so pitiful and sad
It made me feel extremely bad.
My heart was softened to the thing
That asked me if it, please, could sing.
Its little hand I longed to shake,
But, oh, it had no hand to take!
I bent and drew the creature near,
And whispered in its pale blue ear,
"What! Sing, my Cumberbunce? You can!
Sing on, sing loudly, little man!"

The Cumberbunce, without ado,
Gazed sadly on the ocean blue,
And, lifting up its little head,
In tones of awful longing, said:

"Oh, I would sing of mackerel skies,
    And why the sea is wet,
Of jelly-fish and conger-eels,
    And things that I forget.
And I would hum a plaintive tune
    Of why the waves are hot
As water boiling on a stove,
    Excepting that they're not!

"And I would sing of hooks and eyes,
    And why the sea is slant,
And gaily tips the little ships,
    Excepting that I can't!
I never sang a single song,
    I never hummed a note.
There is in me no melody,
    No music in my throat.

A CHRISTMAS DEED OF KINDNESS. *William Heath Robinson* (1872–1944)

FLAT CATS. *Ronald Searle* (1920–)

"So that is why I do not sing
Of sharks, or whales, or anything!"

I looked in innocent surprise,
My wonder showing in my eyes.
"Then why, O, Cumberbunce," I cried,
"Did you come walking at my side
And ask me if you, please, might sing,
When you could not warble anything?"

"I did not ask permission, sir,
I really did not, I aver.
You, sir, misunderstood me, quite.
I did not ask you if I *might*.

Had you correctly understood,
You'd know I asked you if I *could*.
So, as I cannot sing a song,
Your answer, it is plain, was wrong.
The fact I could not sing I knew,
But wanted your opinion, too."

A voice came softly o'er the lea.
"Farewell! my mate is calling me!"

I saw the creature disappear,
Its voice, in parting, smote my ear—
"I thought all people understood
The difference 'twixt 'might' and 'could'!"

Paul West (1871–1918)

MISTRESS DUCK

Good Mistress Duck went out to walk,
With all her boys behind her;
Imagine what their pleasure was
To meet an organ grinder.

H. C. Finlay

TO A CAPTIOUS CRITIC

Dear critic, who my lightness so deplores,
Would I might study to be prince of bores,
Right wisely would I rule that dull estate—
But, sir, I may not, till you abdicate.

Paul Laurence Dunbar (1872–1906)

THE TRUE FACTS OF THE CASE

Once a raven from Pluto's dark shore
Bore the singular news—"Nevermore."
  'Twas of fruitless avail
  To ask further detail—
His reply was the same as before.

Anthony Euwer (1877–1955)

THE FACE

As a beauty I'm not a great star,
There are others more handsome by far,
  But my face I don't mind it,
  Because I'm behind it—
'Tis the folks in the front that I jar.

Anthony Euwer (1877–1955)

LINES FOR CUSCUSCARAWAY AND MIRZA MURAD ALI BEG

How unpleasant to meet Mr. Eliot!
With his features of clerical cut,
And his brow so grim
And his mouth so prim
And his conversation, so nicely
Restricted to What Precisely
And If and Perhaps and But.
How unpleasant to meet Mr. Eliot!
With a bobtail cur
In a coat of fur
And a porpentine cat
And a wopsical hat:
How unpleasant to meet Mr. Eliot!
  (Whether his mouth be open or shut).

T. S. Eliot (1888–1965)

146

LINES AND SQUARES

Whenever I walk in a London street,
I'm ever so careful to watch my feet;
    And I keep in the squares,
    And the masses of bears,

Who wait at the corners all ready to eat
The sillies who tread on the lines of the street,
    Go back to their lairs,
    And I say to them, "Bears,
    Just look how I'm walking in all of the squares!"

And the little bears growl to each other, "He's mine,
As soon as he's silly and steps on a line."
And some of the bigger bears try to pretend
That they came round the corner to look for a friend;
And they try to pretend that nobody cares
Whether you walk on the lines or squares.

But only the sillies believe their talk;
It's ever so 'portant how you walk.
And it's ever so jolly to call out, "Bears,
Just watch me walking in all the squares!"

A. A. Milne (1882–1958)
Illustration by E. H. Shepard (1879–1976)

THE VICAR'S REMORSE

*Having blessed the foxhounds
in accordance with tradition,
he feels the prick of conscience.*

Rea Irvin (1881–1972)

There was an old man went to skate,
And he started at twenty past eight;
At eight twenty-one
All his skating was done,
And they speak of him now as "The Late."

An old man who was asked to play chess,
Said: "I don't know the moves, but I'll guess
I shan't want the king,
He's a useless old thing,
And without him the danger seems less."

R. P. Stone
Illustrations by C. G. Holme (1887–1954)

HOW TO TREAT ELVES

I met an elf-man in the woods,
    The wee-est little elf!
Sitting under a mushroom tall—
    'Twas taller than himself!

"How do you do, little elf," I said,
    "And what do you do all day?"
"I dance 'n fwolic about," said he,
    " 'N scuttle about and play;

"I s'prise the butterflies, 'n when
    A katydid I see,
'Katy didn't!' I say, and he
    Says 'Katy did!' to me!

"I hide behind my mushroom stalk
    When Mister Mole comes froo,
'N only jus' to fwighten him
    I jump out 'n say 'Boo!'

" 'N then I swing on a cobweb swing
    Up in the air so high,
'N the cwickets chirp to hear me sing
    'Upsy-daisy-die!'

" 'N then I play with the baby chicks,
    I call them, chick chick chick!
'N what do you think of that?" said he.
    I said, "It makes me sick.

"It gives me sharp and shooting pains
    To listen to such drool."
I lifted up my foot, and squashed
    The God damn little fool.

Morris Bishop (1893–1973)

BOHEMIA

Authors and actors and artists and such
Never know nothing, and never know much.
Sculptors and singers and those of their kidney
Tell their affairs from Seattle to Sydney.
Playwrights and poets and such horses' necks
Start off from anywhere, end up at sex.
Diarists, critics, and similar roe
Never say nothing, and never say no.
People Who Do Things exceed my endurance;
God, for a man that solicits insurance!

Dorothy Parker (1893–1967)

William Steig (1907–)

Tomi Ungerer (1931–)

PREFACE

Some say the Phœnix dwells in Aethiopia,
In Turkey, Syria, Tartary, or Utopia:
Others assume the continuance of the creature
In unexplored cosmographies of Nature:
One styles it Bird of Paradise; and one
Swears that its nest is built of cinnamon:
While sceptic Eastern Travellers would arraign
The existence of this paragon; and feign
That, since it seems so rare and unprolific,
The bird's a Pseudomorphous Hieroglyphic.

Siegfried Sassoon (1886–1967)

THE PHYSICIAN

. . . . .

He said my cerebellum was brilliant,
And my cerebrum far from N.G.
I know he thought a lot a'
My medulla oblongata,
But he never said he loved me.
He said my maxillaries were marvels,
And found my sternum stunning to see.
He did a double hurdle
When I shook my pelvic girdle,
But he never said he loved me.

He seemed amused
When he first made a test of me
To further his medical art,
Yet he refused
When he'd fix up the rest of me,
To cure that ache in my heart.
I know he thought my pancreas perfect,
And for my spleen was keen as could be,
He said of all his sweeties,
I'd the sweetest diabetes,
But he never said he loved me.

. . . . .

Cole Porter (1893–1964)

GASBAGS

I'm thankful that the sun and moon
Are both hung up so high
That no pretentious hand can stretch
And pull them from the sky.
If they were not, I have no doubt
But some reforming ass
Would recommend to take them down
And light the world with gas.

Anonymous

COUNTESS MITZI

· · · · ·

Beware of Countess Mitzi,
The world will tell you why,
For my name is really
Ludovika—Anastasie—Frederika
Isabel—Rosa—Mariposa
Nikinikolai.
You can perfectly well see why
People think I've a naughty eye
For they'd rather say Countess Mitzi
Just a teensy weensy bitsie
Than a string of names like
Ludovika—Anastasie—Frederika
Isabel—Rosa—Mariposa
Nikinikolai!

Noel Coward (1899–1973)

THE COMMON CORMORANT

The common cormorant (or shag)
Lays eggs inside a paper bag,
You follow the idea, no doubt?
It's to keep the lightning out.
But what these unobservant birds
Have never thought of is that herds
Of wandering bears may come with buns
And steal the bags to hold the crumbs.

Christopher Isherwood (1904–)

THE SHEEP IN WOLF'S CLOTHING

Not very long ago there were two sheep who put on wolf's clothing and went among the wolves as spies, to see what was going on. They arrived on a fete day, when all the wolves were singing in the taverns or dancing in the street. The first sheep said to his companion, "Wolves are just like us, for they gambol and frisk. Every day is fete day in Wolfland." He made some notes on a piece of paper (which a spy should never do) and he headed them "My Twenty-four Hours in Wolfland," for he had decided not to be a spy any longer but to write a book on Wolfland and also some articles for the *Sheep's Home Companion*. The other sheep guessed what he was planning to do, so he slipped away and began to write a book called "My Ten Hours in Wolfland." The first sheep suspected what was up when he found his friend had gone, so he wired a book to his publisher called "My Five Hours in Wolfland," and it was announced for publication first. The other sheep immediately sold his manuscript to a newspaper syndicate for serialization.

Both sheep gave the same message to their fellows: wolves were just like sheep, for they gamboled and frisked, and every day was fete day in Wolfland. The citizens of Sheepland were convinced by all this, so they drew in their sentinels and they let down their barriers. When the wolves descended on them one night, howling and slavering, the sheep were as easy to kill as flies on a windowpane.

Moral: Don't get it right, just get it written.

James Thurber (1894–1961)

THE DOG

The truth I do not stretch or shove
When I state the dog is full of love.
I've also proved, by actual test,
A wet dog is the lovingest.

THE WOMBAT

The wombat lives across the seas,
Among the fair Antipodes.
He may exist on nuts and berries,
Or then again, on missionaries;
His distant habit precludes
Conclusive knowledge of his moods.
But I would not engage the wombat
In any form of mortal combat.

Ogden Nash (1902–1971)
Illustrations by Quentin Blake (1932–)

159

ABOUT CHILDREN

By all the published facts in the case,
Children belong to the human race.

Equipped with consciousness, passions, pulse,
They even grow up and become adults.

So why's the resemblance, moral or mental,
Of children to people so coincidental?

Upright out of primordial dens,
Homo walked and was sapiens.

But rare as leviathans or auks
Is—male or female—the child who walks.

He runs, he gallops, he crawls, he pounces,
Flies, leaps, stands on his head, or bounces,

Imitates snakes or the tiger stripèd
But seldom recalls he is labeled "Biped."

Which man or woman have you set sights on
Who craves to slumber with all the lights on

Yet creeps away to a lampless nook
In order to pore on a comic book?

Why, if (according to A. Gesell)
The minds of children ring clear as a bell,

Does every question one asks a tot
Receive the similar answer—"What?"

And who ever started the baseless rumor
That any child has a sense of humor?

Children conceive of no jest that's madder
Then Daddy falling from a ten-foot ladder.

Their fancies sway like jetsam and flotsam;
One minute they're winsome, the next they're swatsome.

While sweet their visages, soft their arts are,
Cold as a mermaiden's kiss their hearts are;

They comprehend neither pity nor treason.
An hour to them is a three months' season.

So who can say—this is just between us—
That children and we are a common genus,

When the selfsame nimbus is eerily worn
By a nymph, a child, and a unicorn?

Phyllis McGinley (1905–1978)
Illustrations by Roberta MacDonald

FOUR LITTLE TIGERS

Four little tigers
Sitting in a tree;
One became a lady's coat—
Now there's only three.

Three little tigers
'Neath a sky of blue;
One became a rich man's rug—
Now there's only two.

Two little tigers
Sleeping in the sun;
One a hunter's trophy made—
Now there's only one.

One little tiger
Waiting to be had;
Oops! He got the hunter first—
Aren't you kind of glad?

SING A SONG
OF SPILLAGE

Sing a song of spillage—
A tanker's fouled the shore;
Four-and-twenty black birds—
They were white before.

WEE WILLIE WINKIE

Wee Willie Winkie
Guns up and down
On his souped-up Harley,
Waking up the town;
If you think that Willie
Makes a racket, Mister,
Wait till Willie's brother
Turns on his transistor.

LITTLE BO-PEEP

Little Bo-Peep
Has lost her sheep
And thinks they may be roaming;
They haven't fled;
They've all dropped dead
　　From nerve gas in Wyoming.

Frank Jacobs
Illustrations by Paul Coker, Jr.

MEANWHILE

Here we are at st custards poised between past and future. How far along the road hav we traveled? How far must we proceed? Wot of Livy and J. Caesar? Will Bluebell win the 2.30 at Kempton? Who cares? This is the present and it is up to us to make it as beauteous as possible.

Geoffrey Willans and Ronald Searle (1920–)

AXIOM TO GRIND

Vice
Is nice
But a little virtue
Won't hurt you.

Felicia Lamport (1916–)
Illustration by
Edward Gorey (1925–)

Having mentioned laughing, I must particularly warn
you against it; and I could heartily wish that you may
often be seen to smile, but never heard to laugh, while
you live. Frequent and loud laughter is the character-
istic of folly and ill manners: it is the manner in
which the mob express their silly joy at silly things,
and they call it being merry. In my mind there is
nothing so illiberal and so ill-bred as audible laughter.

Lord Chesterfield (1694–1773)

Acknowledgments

Grateful acknowledgment is made to the following for permission to reprint copyrighted material:

The Bodley Head: Selections from *The Old Man Book,* text by R. P. Stone, illustrations by C. G. Holme.

Curtis Brown Limited and the Estate of E. C. Bentley: The verse "Columbus" by Edmund Clerihew Bentley, from *More Biography* by E. C. Bentley.

Diogenes Verlag AG: "Cat with Sardine Can," from *Compromises* by Tomi Ungerer. Copyright © 1970 by Diogenes Verlag AG, Zurich.

Dodd, Mead & Company, Inc.: "To a Captious Critic," from *The Complete Poems of Paul Laurence Dunbar.*

Doubleday & Company, Inc.; The National Trust; and A. P. Watt Ltd.: "The Butterfly that Stamped," from *Rudyard Kipling's Verse: Definitive Edition.*

Gerald Duckworth & Co. Ltd.: "Algernon," "Rebecca," and "Jim," from *Cautionary Tales* by Hilaire Belloc, 1908.

E. P. Dutton, Inc.; McClelland and Stewart Limited; Curtis Brown Limited, London; and Methuen & Co. Ltd., London: The poem "Lines and Squares" and illustration from *When We Were Very Young* by A. A. Milne. Copyright 1924 by E. P. Dutton & Co., Inc. Copyright renewed 1952 by A. A. Milne.

E. C. Publications, Inc./Mad Magazine: "Sing a Song of Spillage," "Wee Willie Winkie," "Four Little Tigers," and "Little Bo Peep," from *Mad About the Buoy* (*Mad's Ecology Mother Goose*), text by Frank Jacobs and illustrations by Paul Coker, Jr. Copyright © 1972 by E. C. Publications, Inc.

Farrar, Straus and Giroux, Inc.: "Clown and bird play trumpets," from *Drawings* by William Steig. Copyright © 1974, 1979 by William Steig.

Edward Gorey and Felicia Lamport: "Axiom to Grind," from *Scrap Irony.* Illustration by Edward Gorey, text by Felicia Lamport.

Harcourt Brace Jovanovich, Inc.: "On a Flimmering Floom You Shall Ride" by Carl Sandburg, from *The Complete Poems of Carl Sandburg.* Copyright 1950 by Carl Sandburg; copyright 1978 by Margaret Sandburg, Helga Sandburg Crile, and Janet Sandburg.

Harcourt Brace Jovanovich, Inc., and Faber & Faber Limited: "Lines for Cuscuscaraway and Mirza Murad Ali Beg," from *Collected Poems 1909–1962* by T. S. Eliot, copyright 1936 by Harcourt Brace Jovanovich, Inc.; copyright © 1963, 1964 by T. S. Eliot.

Christopher Isherwood: "The Common Cormorant or Shag" by Christopher Isherwood.

Ladies' Home Journal: "The Wash That Stayed Out All Night" by Oliver Herford, from the April 1927 issue of *Ladies' Home Journal.* Copyright 1927 by Ladies' Home Journal Publishing Inc.

Little, Brown and Company; Curtis Brown Limited; and A. P. Watt Ltd.: "The Dog," from *Everyone but Thee and Me* by Ogden Nash. Copyright © 1962 by Ogden Nash. "The Wombat," from *Verses from 1926 On* by Ogden Nash. Copyright 1933 by The Curtis Publishing Company. Two illustrations from *Custard and Company* by Ogden Nash. Poems selected and illustrated by Quentin Blake. Copyright © 1980 by Quentin Blake.

The Morgan Library: "The Dog in the Manger," from *Bennett's Fables.*

The New Yorker Magazine, Inc.: Drawing by Rea Irvin from the December 5, 1931, issue of *The New Yorker.* Copyright © 1931, 1959 by The New Yorker Magazine, Inc.

Index OF TITLES

Index OF AUTHORS AND ILLUSTRATORS

Pages in italics refer to illustrations.

$\mathscr{Index}$ OF FIRST LINES